The Revd Dr Liz Hoare is 1
Hall, Oxford. Prior to this,
parishes in Yorkshire, and was among the first women to be ordained
priest in the Church of England in 1994. Liz has been giving and
receiving spiritual direction since her early twenties and has wide
experience of different styles of directing. She has also co-led two
training courses for spiritual directors in the York diocese. Liz has a
PhD in Tudor history from the University of Durham. She is married
to a retired parish priest who is also a sculptor and they have one
son who recently became a teenager. In her spare time, Liz enjoys
birdwatching and bread-making and belongs to a lively book group
for discussing the novels she loves to read.

USING THE BIBLE IN SPIRITUAL DIRECTION

Liz Hoare

Foreword by Daniel L. Prechtel

Morehouse Publishing
NEW YORK

First published in Great Britain in 2015

Society for Promoting Christian Knowledge
36 Causton Street
London SW1P 4ST
www.spck.org.uk

First published in the United States in 2016 by
Morehouse Publishing, 19 East 34th Street, New York, NY 10016
Morehouse Publishing is an imprint of Church Publishing Incorporated.
www.churchpublishing.org

Cover design by Linda Brooks
Typeset by Graphicraft Limited, Hong Kong

Library of Congress Cataloging-in-Publication Data
A catalog record of this book is available from the Library of Congress.
ISBN-13: 978-0-8192-3257-1 (pbk.)
ISBN-13: 978-0-8192-3258-8 (ebook)

Printed in the United States of America

For Jan

Contents

Foreword

If we extended St. Brigid's quip that "a person without a soul friend is like a body without a head," we could say that a Christian without the Bible is like a body without a heart. Someone who wants a deep spiritual life as a Christian will draw vital assistance from both a spiritual director (soul friend) and the support and guidance of Holy Scriptures.

We can be grateful for the expanding availability of spiritual directors over the past thirty years so that now virtually everyone, whether affiliated with a religious tradition or not, who wishes a spiritual guide has the opportunity to meet with someone either individually or in a group setting, in person or with the help of long-distance technologies. Awareness of the benefits of spiritual direction have expanded from Roman Catholic and Anglican (Episcopal) traditions into many Protestant Christian denominations, as well as other non-Christian religious traditions, and to those who are independent spiritual sojourners.

Training programs and theological education courses in the art of spiritual direction have proliferated over this period to meet the growing demand. Many programs equip their students for a spiritual direction ministry in a Christian ecumenical environment; and some programs now prepare their students for interfaith spiritual direction. I have had the privilege of helping shape new spiritual directors in both ecumenical and interfaith settings.

However, as North American programs for spiritual directors expand into broader and more diverse contexts, the need also increases for solid information that gives students an orientation to the Bible, approaches to interpreting scripture, and its use for the ongoing spiritual formation of Christians. Those who enter training as spiritual directors, as gifted as they are, may not have much personal experience or educational background in reading and interpreting scripture and praying with it.

Certainly, those who are seeking ongoing guidance and reflection as Christians deserve competent spiritual directors that are aware of the importance of the Bible and how it can be used well for their client's spiritual benefit. The Bible is, after all, the primary source for shaping Jewish and Christian understandings of God's revelations to humanity; including the crucial stories of Jesus' life, teachings, ministry, crucifixion, and resurrection. The Church calls the Bible "Holy Scriptures" and "the Word of God" because "God inspired their human authors and because God still speaks to us through the Bible" (1979 *Book of Common Prayer*, 853). So it is imperative that those who offer spiritual companionship to Christians have a solid understanding of the Bible and its use for discerning God's voice and guidance.

Consequently, the Rev. Dr. Liz Hoare's book, *Using the Bible in Spiritual Direction*, comes to us now as an essential resource for the formation of new spiritual directors, and as a valuable guide for those who already are practitioners. This edition by Morehouse Publishing for a North American audience is being released alongside the original British edition by SPCK. *Using the Bible in Spiritual Direction* provides a solid foundation for spiritual direction that is rooted in models drawn from Holy Scriptures and the developing Christian experience of spiritual guidance and formation. It provides practical information on the use of the Bible alongside addressing important themes and issues related to interpretation and approach. Liz Hoare successfully brings head and heart together in the service of Christian spiritual guidance and practice.

Daniel L. Prechtel

The Rev. Dr. Daniel L. Prechtel is an Episcopal priest, educator, and spiritual director. He teaches and supervises for spiritual direction training programs and seminary courses since 1996. He is the author of *Where Two or Three are Gathered: Spiritual Direction for Small Groups.*

Preface

Recently I had a holiday in South Africa with my family. The first week was spent with friends who had a house there and knew the local area well. They guided us on safari, taught us important safety rules, took us to places where we could watch the animals to best advantage, often well off the beaten track, introduced us to some local residents and told us stories of their own adventures. After that we hired a car and drove the famous Garden Route on our own. Keeping to the main roads, we stayed in B & Bs, explored with the aid of maps and guide books and covered many miles. It was a very different experience and we knew we were only skimming the surface of the landscape. Many Christians long for a deeper, richer experience of God of the kind that comes from being at home in his presence at every moment. Richard Foster, the American writer on spirituality, described superficiality as the curse of our age and called for Christians to show the way by moving beyond surface living into the depths.[1] Being with our friends in South Africa enabled us to feel at home and to understand more deeply the way of life there.

The Bible describes a person who is a Christian as someone whose life is 'hidden with Christ in God' (Col. 3.3). In 2 Corinthians 5.17, Paul wrote that 'if anyone is in Christ, there is a new creation', and frequently referred to being 'in Christ' as the way to knowing God. There is a sense of inhabiting a new landscape, of being so immersed in God that we see the world with new eyes and experience the reality of the words 'In him we live and move and have our being' (Acts 17.28). If the purpose of Christian discipleship is to become more like the Christ we seek to follow, so that we may know God and find our home in fellowship with the Trinity, the purpose of spiritual direction may be said to assist us in this goal. The underlying premise of this book is that knowing God as God speaks to us in the Scriptures will help us recognize God's voice as we go about our daily lives.

The reaction to hearing that I was writing about using the Bible in spiritual direction has been revealing. One person was surprised and could not see what the Bible had to do with spiritual direction. Another confessed how much she wished there had been some Bible in her training as a director. Some who hold the Bible in high regard but are wary of spiritual direction are eager to see what the word of God has to say about this area. Others who are experienced directors have asked helpful questions about what this would look like in practice.

This is a book about the practice of spiritual direction. Its aim is to show the part played by the Scriptures in this ancient ministry. The aim of spiritual direction is to hear and respond to God. In classical Christianity, spiritual direction stands within a tradition. It is understood as a gift given by the Spirit to the Church and exercised by individuals within the body of Christ. It is available to all Christians to help us inhabit God's landscape more fully and discover where our treasure lies. It is arguably needed in today's Church more than ever before. At a time when the Church is haemorrhaging members at an alarming rate, the demand for spiritual directors continues to rise. This bears out research that suggests that although people have lost confidence in institutional religion, they have not abandoned faith – far from it. Demand for spiritual directors outstrips supply. For many people spiritual direction is perceived as a ministry that offers nurture and a way to keep the flame of faith alive. Christian discipleship is not a matter of acquiring a set of skills to make us proficient in the Christian way. It is about the formation of Christian character. This is a lifelong process. Spiritual direction is concerned with walking the way with people who are exploring faith and seeking spiritual maturity. In all that follows, the Christian Scriptures are understood to have a privileged place within the Christian tradition and to be authoritative for all Christians, including spiritual directors and those they direct. The question of course is how that plays out in the context of spiritual direction. When Jesus was teaching his disciples he told them to store up for themselves treasure in heaven because, he said, 'where your treasure is, there your heart will be also' (Matt. 6.21).

The aim of this book is to show that the simple yet profound gift of Christians ministering to one another through the art of spiritual direction is all about the work of the Holy Spirit who works in as many ways as there are human beings, often mysteriously and always to bring us to Jesus Christ who is the living Word. Spiritual direction is a means, not an end, to making us complete in God (Phil. 1.6). I have written both for people who give spiritual direction and also those who receive it. Within a pluralist, consumer-dominated climate, spirituality is often perceived as an accessory. I am not trying to suggest that spiritual direction is one more product that we might try for a while to see if we like it. It is an ancient practice that has much to offer the Christian Church today, but it is not being promoted as an add-on. It is most definitely not a self-improvement programme. We are created to know and love God. Jesus calls us to take up our cross and follow him, and we can only do this if we know and love him and look forward to serving him in this life and to being with him for ever in the next one. The call to every disciple, however, is to follow Christ, not to have a spiritual director. The place of the Scriptures in the Christian life, on the other hand, is not optional, though there are many different ways of approaching them. The word of God is as life and breath to Christian believers, and as such is a *sine qua non* of the Christian life. Spiritual direction is one way to help maintain the centrality of the word of God in the DNA of God's children, so that we may learn to recognize the living Word in the written word speaking directly to us. It is in that spirit that this book has been written.

1

Introduction: What is spiritual direction?

I was hungry for God in my early twenties. I bought a book with that very title, hoping that reading would lead me in the right direction as it so often had before.[1] When someone suggested spiritual direction, I had no idea what it was but was willing to try anything that might answer my spiritual desire for more. My first director was a male priest who sat behind his desk and listened to my faltering description of how I prayed. It was a very old-fashioned approach, but it sustained me enough to seek another director when he moved away. This time it was a very different approach, though with the same aim as before. My director, a lay woman, listened as we sat together in her sitting room, and occasionally interjected with a well-placed question. At the end she would gather up all the fragments of conversation and offer it to God with me. Since then I have had a number of spiritual directors from different spiritual traditions, all of whom have offered me hospitality and time in which to have a conversation about where God is at work in my life.

Spiritual direction is a <u>relational ministry</u> between two people whereby both are seeking to listen to the Holy Spirit. Directors make themselves available to those seeking direction, offering prayerful support and encouragement to help them listen and respond to God. It is God the Holy Spirit, in fact, who is the real director, so the essential foundation of spiritual direction is a three-way relationship. From the start there are three persons involved in this shared conversation, for conversation is the stuff of spiritual direction. The term describes a structured ministry of listening and spiritual formation on the part of the director, with the aim of enabling another Christian to grow in relationship with God and in obedience to God. A typical meeting for spiritual direction will last about an hour, and frequency of meetings can vary considerably. Often when a person is just beginning, there may be shorter gaps between meetings, perhaps four to six weeks. Later on many people find that three or four times a year is sufficient, especially if they have to travel some distance to see their director. Some relationships last for years and grow through many changes, but no one should feel tied to the same director for life. When embarking on spiritual direction for the first time, both sides involved should feel free to explore possibilities and say if they feel things are not a good 'fit'. Finding a director may be a challenge. Some Anglican dioceses hold lists of names of people who have undergone some training and/or have the reputation of being good directors, but often it is word of mouth that really counts. 'When you find a good person, make tracks to his door' is wise advice, and matters more than any courses completed, though these help to hone skills that may be already latent.

Signposts and guides

Throughout the story of God's involvement with humanity, one person has been used time and time again to point the way to another. The Bible, the Christian Scriptures, tell the story of this relationship between God and the world. In both Old and New Testaments we see instances of spiritual direction taking place, and we will examine some of these in the course of the book. In particular we will explore how the Gospels depict Jesus in his relationships with those he encounters, for above all he shows us the way to the Father and the way to live well.

With the birth of the Christian Church at Pentecost, the good news about Jesus began to spread, and in the book of Acts and the epistles we see how the first Christians learned how to put into practice what they had heard and understood about him. Christian faith according to the New Testament is something to believe and also something to do. It involves a new way to understand ourselves and who we are and also a new way to live. Most of the letters in the New Testament are written to churches, and the Gospels are understood to have arisen out of Christian communities. Between the Gospels and the letters is the Acts of the Apostles, which is the story of the early Church. We see that discipleship is something learned alongside others and that often it involves one Christian guiding another on the way. Indeed those first Christians were known as people of the Way. It is helpful to regard the 'direction' part of spiritual direction as a signpost along the way rather than as one person telling another what to do. Spiritual direction is not in the least about handing over responsibility for our lives to another human being. Keeping the Scriptures central to spiritual direction is an important means for both director and directee to remember this vital point. God desires that we should grow to be mature men and women, not kept in bondage to someone else's agenda or subservient to someone else's power.

'Spiritual' direction?

The term 'spiritual' is open to so many interpretations that many people feel that talking about 'spiritual direction' is altogether too confusing. 'Spiritual' may suggest the non-physical world but spiritual direction is concerned with the whole of life. The focus in direction is on prayer but that does not mean that only prayer is talked about – we do not pray in a vacuum. There is a story of a Russian *staretz*, or holy man, who was criticized for spending so long talking with an old woman – who had come to him for spiritual direction – about her turkeys. 'But her whole life is in those turkeys', was his response. Spiritual direction is for people who want to know God in their daily lives, whatever it involves and however mundane it may seem. Finding God in the ordinary is fundamental to knowing God personally and learning to hear God's voice. Spiritual direction embraces the totality of life, and this is far more important than whether we are using a particular method or following a defined tradition.

The New Testament helps us to get a better understanding of the word 'spiritual' in the context of spiritual direction. When the apostle Paul writes about the spiritual life he uses the word *pneuma* and contrasts it with the flesh, or *sarx*, meaning life without Christ or the old self. *Sarx* is sometimes referred to as the false self as it involves a way of living that is inauthentic. This false self desires independence from God and struggles against surrender to God's rule. One writer has described this false self as a fearful, protective, possessive, manipulative, destructive, self-promoting, indulgent, distinction-making self. The Christian life is about the transformation of this old self into the mature human beings that we are meant to be. For all of us there is work to be done regarding the old self![2]

It is in the pages of the Scriptures that we find the antidote to the false self in the goal of the spiritual life. When Paul refers to the spiritual as opposed to the flesh, he was thinking of the whole of a person rightly related to God from their inner being, or hidden self or heart, where Christ dwells through his Spirit (1 Cor. 2.6–10). We are destined to be like Christ himself, conformed to his image, being changed little by little into his likeness (cf. 2 Cor. 3.18). God first of all came and shared our life in order to redeem us. 'The Word became flesh and lived among us' – or as the Greek literally translated means, 'pitched his tent among us' (John 1.14). It can be the experience of every Christian that God still comes to share our lives, but the goal is ultimately to be transformed into God's own likeness. That will look different for every believer, for each one of us relates to God out of the unique way we are created, and it is the reason that the Bible does not simply set out a single blueprint for every person to copy. The task of spiritual direction is to understand what this work of transformation means in a person's unique life and experience.

It is as we seek God that we discover our true identity. Even though spiritual direction involves us talking about ourselves, the focus is God and God's action in our lives. As C. S. Lewis explained in *Mere Christianity*: 'Your real new self . . . will not come as long as you are looking for it. It will come when you are looking for Him.'[3] This is a lifelong process – the journey of life. Spiritual direction is just one way of enabling us to pay attention to the process of becoming like Christ and to learn how to live out of our true centre – that is, Christ – rather than our own selves, but its integrative nature is one of its supreme benefits for anyone wanting to take seriously the day-by-day process.

Spiritual direction and today's spirituality

'Spirituality' is a term closely connected to this context, and we will use it frequently in these pages. It is a word that has become common currency in Western culture and, like 'spiritual', is open to wide interpretation. The dominant motif in the Western world is a marketplace spirituality with tempting offers, over-the-top promises, busyness and bustle, initiatives and performance factors all built in. It is full of options because it is a commodity where choice and individuality reign supreme. Much of what passes for spirituality today is less and less connected with the Christian tradition. Hence this book. Christian spirituality, properly understood, is nothing like the privatized, personal therapies designed to cultivate the self vying for attention in our culture. Given all this, 'spirituality' requires a working definition for its use here. At its most basic it can be understood as 'lived experience', but as with 'spiritual', it will be helpful to give it some clearer Christian content. It may be thought of as living out what I believe about God, Father, Son and Holy Spirit. This roots it in a theological context and also in that lived experience already referred to here. Spiritual direction is essentially a ministry of integration as it brings together spirituality with psychology, soul care – or pastoral ministry – and theology. It is not psychotherapy with a pinch of mysticism thrown in.

Terminology

I have decided to retain the term 'spiritual direction' for a number of reasons. First, it resonates across the Christian Church. Second, it connects the contemporary practice of spiritual direction with its long and established history in the Church. Third, properly understood, the word 'direction' vividly describes the practice of pointing the way to all Christian pilgrims. While the notion of journey has also become somewhat hackneyed, it is a deeply biblical theme in both Old and New Testaments and has meaning for countless Christians seeking to travel through life with Christ and who see themselves as pilgrims. 'Spiritual direction' as a description of journeying with others in prayer thus has a robustness about it and offers the opportunity to rescue the true meaning of both words in a biblical way. Using 'spiritual' in the way that the Scriptures use it challenges the hijacking of its meaning by those who want to empty it of its Christian context, while focusing on the signposting angle of 'direction' can enable both director and directee to remain dependent on Christ at all times.

Retaining the word 'director' raises the stakes in what can be expected from going to talk to one on a regular basis, and this will be explored in the chapters that follow. Determinedly hands-off directors are nevertheless seeking to point us to Christ, and besides offering the space to be in and the time to sit and talk or be still, all with unconditional acceptance, are there to be an icon of Christ to those before them. An icon is not the object of devotion per se but rather conveys something of Christ to the one gazing at it. St Paul wrote of the way that God has 'shone in our hearts to give the light of the knowledge of the glory of God in the face of Jesus Christ' and how we are carrying this treasure within us 'in clay jars, so that it may be made clear that this extraordinary power belongs to God and does not come from us' (2 Cor. 4.6–7).[4] There will be times when directees need direction in terms of spiritual wisdom. They need to know that the director is praying for them as well as listening with 'an understanding heart' (1 Kings 3.9 KJV; cf. 'understanding mind' NRSV). They may also need reassurance that God is still there, and look for such reassurance in the stance of the director. They will certainly want the director to be open to the Spirit and to exercise discernment.

The renewal of spiritual direction in the twentieth century

When Kenneth Leech wrote his important book *Soul Friend* in 1977, he surveyed the current scene of spiritual searching in Western society. It was a time when many Christians were turning to Buddhism, Transcendental Meditation and Eastern mysticism in search of meaning and depth. The charismatic movement was in full swing and various radical theologies, not least liberation theology, were emerging. Leech noted three broad movements in operation: first, a search for the inner world of meditation, silence and contemplative prayer; second, a sense of the need for power and direct experience of the Holy Spirit; third, an increasing sense of the need to see the search for justice as an integral part of the gospel. There is little overt mention of the Bible in Leech's analysis of the Church's response, though he noted a sense of the Bible having 'come alive' for many affected by the charismatic movement, and he concluded that all three movements were in urgent need at that time of the orientation that spiritual direction could give. The inner search would end up in a blind alley with no help to interpret the experiences undergone, the charismatic movement risked leaving people in the place of darkness following peak experiences with little hope of spiritual progress, while the radical Christians involved in social and political issues could easily lose touch with their spiritual roots. Shallowness and rootlessness seemed to pervade the religious scene, and for Leech the main hope lay in personal guidance that took the form of spiritual direction. He declared passionately that: 'Never was spiritual direction more urgently called for than in the present climate of soul searching.'[5]

Leech's understanding of spiritual direction is firmly within the classical tradition of spiritual growth and spiritual guidance that is rooted in the Scriptures. He considers it to be an integral part of the pastoral work to which every priest is called, and that it arises out of prayer, study and ascetical theology.[6] Leech's insistence that there is an inseparable link between doctrine and spirituality needs emphasizing. He reminds us that pastoral care and the cure of souls derive their dual emphasis of care and healing from Scripture. The Latin *cura* primarily means care but can also mean healing, and both ideas are held together in the image of the Shepherd, who is the one who feeds and nourishes the flock, strengthens the weak, seeks the lost, cares for the sick and binds up the wounded (Ezek. 34.3–4; 15–16). Ezekiel's model of the Shepherd is also concerned with the achievement of *shalom* (34.24). The New Testament builds on this, bringing together the themes of the wounded healer, the slain lamb, the stricken shepherd and the guide who nourishes the flock. Linking the work of the spiritual director to the work of the priest is an important reminder that spiritual direction is a ministry for the Church and exercised on behalf of the Church. It is, as Leech concludes, 'within the common life of the flock and of the Body that the work of spiritual theology takes place'.[7]

Like so many writers before and since who address the subject of spiritual direction, Kenneth Leech, himself an ordained priest, could take for granted a framework of Christian belief and faith that was everywhere implied. Biblical allusions, themes and narratives as well as discussion of theological concepts did not need explaining because these writers assumed their readers would know immediately to what they referred. Increasingly that is no longer the case. We no longer view the world through the lens of the Bible in the way previous generations did, even those among them who did not regard themselves as active Christians. Much has changed since biblical phrases pervaded common speech and the Christian Church had a much stronger hold on society than it does today. Yet Leech's predictions that spiritual direction would become more important have become reality. This requires some explanation.

Today's spiritual climate

The renewal of spiritual direction has taken place alongside social and cultural developments of the modern and postmodern world that affect us all. One of the reasons for the explosion of interest in spiritual direction is the enlarged understanding of what it means to be human through the development of the human sciences. Spiritual direction has learned a great deal about what goes on when one person talks and the other listens. Until the 1960s most spiritual direction was given to priests and people in the religious life by other priests and monks and nuns. It was also largely the preserve of the Roman Catholic Church and was certainly not something those outside the catholic tradition would consider as a means of spiritual growth. The ecumenical movement and the Second Vatican Council brought huge changes to the Church in the West and to the way Christians related to one another. Retreats and spiritual direction began to open up to lay men and women and not only to those from the catholic tradition. The retreat movement today counts Baptists, Methodists, Anglicans, Quakers and others among its members, many of whom have a spiritual director in addition to going away on retreat. There are training courses for people who feel called to this ministry, and many who practise are lay people. Some of the most popular courses in theology are those concerning spirituality and spiritual direction. There is an ever-growing number of books on the subject. Despite the training courses on offer, however, the demand for spiritual directors outweighs their availability. The renaissance of spiritual direction is something to be celebrated in the Church today. It represents a desire to know God, a desire to grow in the spiritual life, and is a healthy check on the general doom and gloom expressed concerning the state of the Church in the West. In the words of Gary W. Moon and David G. Benner in their book *Spiritual Direction and the Care of Souls*, the rediscovery of spiritual direction represents for many 'the recovery of the lost jewel in the crown of Christian soul care'.[8]

Spiritual direction today

Spiritual direction has ancient roots but it has also undergone change and development during its long history. Today it thrives in the Western Church in the mindset of a therapeutic culture. It has gained fresh insights from the world of counselling and therapy but it is neither of these in essence. Everywhere we look there are those who claim to have discovered the meaning of life, how to be happy and how to succeed. Questions about what life is for continue to exercise us as human beings whoever we are. We can choose to consult a life coach, a counsellor, a psychotherapist, even a hypnotist to enable us to discover our true potential. Spiritual directors may find themselves described as mentors, counsellors, guides or friends, and all of these suggest different models of operating; but spiritual direction remains something different from all these in and of itself. The main difference between spiritual direction and all other forms of talking therapies is that its purpose is focused on the person and on what God is doing in that person's life, so that he or she may be formed into the likeness of Christ. Spiritual direction helps us pay attention to what God is saying to us through our everyday experience, which includes prayer and listening to the word. What this looks like in practice will be different for different individuals, but what it means in essence is that God's agenda, not my agenda, is the focus of what goes on. This is deeply reassuring for anyone involved in spiritual direction, either in the giving or the receiving of it. While the relationship between the director and directee is important to the extent that it can make or break the experience of direction, it is not the point of the encounter. The director's primary task, in fact, is to get out of the way so that directees may hear the word of the Lord speaking to them.

Focus on experience

A further development in the practice of spiritual direction during the second half of the twentieth century was the shift in focus from keeping rules to reflecting on experience. In a postmodern world, experience is everything and it is valid because it is personal. My experience may be different from yours but I cannot challenge the truth of your experience any more than you can mine. At the same time much modern philosophy has been preoccupied with the question of whether we can experience anything outside ourselves. It seems a purely subjective thing, as indicated just now. How is it possible to discern whether someone's experience of God is real or not? Yet spiritual direction not only centres on human experience but on personal experience of a God who acts in the world in such a way that we may experience that action. The overall aim of spiritual direction is to help those seeking God to pay attention to their whole experience of life to understand where God is at work and so discern the next step of faith. We need a theology of the spiritual life and of spiritual direction that takes into account God's action in the world in a way that grounds the practice of prayer and the work of spiritual direction. What part do the Scriptures play in this? The premise underlying this book is that God has made God's self known in God's word, and that this is foundational to the ministry of spiritual direction. We cannot practise discernment unless we have a growing understanding of who God is and how God acts in the world.[9]

Experience and the Bible

The psalmist says 'you have set my feet in a broad place' (Ps. 31.8). To regard the Scriptures as the locus of God's self-revelation is in no way to close down the importance of experience or to argue that one must trump the other. Spiritual direction is about God and my experience in conversation. Directors and directees may have different theological perspectives and different degrees of awareness and ability to articulate theological concepts, but in Christian spiritual direction there is an assumption that both will share the Jesus story and the Christian creeds. Within this there needs to be room to move about, to breathe freely and to explore. If our theologies are too narrow, we may miss what God is up to in a person's life. Directors need to be open to having their theological horizons broadened as they listen to the experiences of God in the lives of those they direct. They need to be able to hold the range of ways of attending to Scripture across the various Christian traditions so that they can draw on appropriate verses and passages in ways that enable the directee to hear. The directee is seeking help to interpret their experience and so meet God in new ways. Directors need to ask themselves 'What counts as religious experience?' – for their directees will almost certainly be asking this. Do ordinary non-religious values and attitudes such as courage, selflessness and endurance count? And if so, how might they help us discern the work of the Spirit in us? How might they lead to a deeper experience of God? The Scriptures can help to guide our reflections here. They work not in isolation but hand in hand with recognition and gratitude for God's presence, the gentle but persistent questioning of a supportive director, the community of faith to which one belongs and the ongoing reflection of the person who is seeking.

2

Learning to reflect on our experience

Paying attention

In seeking God and paying attention to what the living Word is saying, we encounter grace. 'What is the grace that I need today?' is a simple question that St Ignatius encouraged people to ask as they reflected on the day that has been and look forward to tomorrow. Grace is a religious word, yet most of us recognize it when we receive it, whether or not we would call ourselves Christians.

The Roman Catholic theologian Karl Rahner argued that grace is always something that is experienced. For him the essence of grace is 'the self-communication of God to the transcendent spirit of [men and women]'.[1] This experience of grace draws people to God in knowledge and love. It is of course the action of God in a person that enables them to experience grace in the first place. It takes people out of a purely intellectual approach to faith into reflection on actual experience, the experience of the touch of God in our lives.

Our experience is always shaped by the language we use to describe it. 'Raw' experience as such does not exist, for as soon as we try to put into words what we have experienced we have begun to interpret it. Spiritual direction involves conversation and conversation involves listening to people, not just to utterances. This includes the words we choose to say and those we choose not to say. The silences are important, pauses that may be pregnant with meaning as we listen to what is not said. There are many silences in Scripture that are worthy of attention. Body language is important for it is one of the most revealing ways we communicate. Our bodies may say far more about how we are feeling deep down than our words could ever articulate. Although the Bible is at first glance words on a page, it contains much in the way of human communication through body language. We are told to 'taste and see that the LORD is good' (Ps. 34.8), for example. Every human emotion is represented in the Psalms, often expressed in the raw, but when the psalmist wants to convey contented trust in God, a metaphor is the best way to express it: 'I have calmed and quieted my soul, like a weaned child with its mother' (Ps. 131.2). We read of weeping and tears, of dancing with joy, of the grinding of teeth and the burning fire within.

Spiritual directors need to feel at ease if the person before them wants to describe their experience in ways that do not comply with creeds or religious formulae. Conversation makes room for difference and listening to other perspectives. Directees may not wish to hear what light Scripture could shed on their experience either, at least not in the rawness of their experience. That may come later and requires discernment as to when and how. It is important that we begin the process of making sense of experience in the light of the Scriptures and the Christian tradition for growth into the likeness of Christ, but we need to be able to move out of the story from time to time in order to return to take our place within it once more. This will be especially important for anyone who has been battered by an experience of any kind of abuse, including use of the Bible.

Challenge from within the Christian tradition

Janet Ruffing, a teacher and practitioner of spiritual direction, argues that it makes a difference whether or not we name something within the Christian tradition.[2] It deepens our appreciation of the tradition and becomes more than something to which we give intellectual assent. It may help us with those aspects of faith that we struggle with because as we experience its reality for ourselves, we are able to imagine what it has been like for others to know it to be true. We are enabled to feel more connected to the body of Christ. We discover that to believe is not to lose our individuality or our unique experience of God. Christian faith is big enough to encompass a multitude of personal encounters with the mysteries of faith. It can cope with struggle, doubts and challenges.

Occasionally I meet people who seem to be afraid of new experiences in case they rock the boat of their belief system. They are right to suspect that this is often the case, but if the root of the disturbance is God, they do not need to be afraid. God will shatter the idols we construct one way or another in order for us to grow as humans. To grow means that our vision of God will need to expand. C. S. Lewis put profound words into the mouth of the Christ figure Aslan the lion speaking to Lucy in *Prince Caspian* when he said: 'every year you grow, you will find me bigger'.[3] We discover that God is always one step ahead, urging us to catch a bigger vision of God's ways. Encountering people who are different from ourselves, venturing out of our securities to help someone, losing a loved one, undergoing the breakup of a relationship will all cause us to question accepted ideas about how things should be. Sometimes it is in the realm of ideas – climate change, the new cosmology, a breakthrough in understanding the human brain. If we allow ourselves to reflect, the chances are we will have to revise some of our ideas about God and the way the world is.

Experience, as already suggested, may be positive or negative. Positive experiences are those that evoke a sense of being loved by God through the love of another person, or the wonder of life through seeing a beautiful landscape. Rahner describes the negative experiences as the 'cracks' in our interpretations and encounters. Such cracks are those times when 'everyday realities break and dissolve'. Disappointment, being betrayed or let down and so on are negative experiences. Where may we find light to help us make sense of them? The experiences discussed by Rahner cannot be accounted for by natural goodness, optimism or kindness. Instead they disclose the mystery that is God to us. They indicate theological virtues – faith, hope, love and so on – that are emerging in us by the power of the Holy Spirit. It may be that through spiritual direction someone who is manifesting such grace needs to hear that they are hereby demonstrating the life of Christ shining through them. Being helped to notice can then lead on to reflection and a deepening of the experience of God. Here reflection with the help of the Scriptures can root directees more deeply within the Christian faith and reassure them they are indeed travelling in the right direction. I have found that a desire to forgive and a desire to say thank you are two of the most common experiences that lead people who would not consider themselves to be card-carrying Christians to think about the possibility that God may be real and personal.

Articulating our experience

For those who have no landscape of faith to which to relate their experience, there may be a struggle to find words that enable them to articulate what has gone on. One of the central tasks of spiritual direction is helping people to articulate how they experience God. Our culture no longer helps us in the way it once did through Sunday School and RE in schools that rendered Bible stories accessible. Biblical language that was formerly embedded in the culture is less and less explicit. Who could imagine a politician proclaiming 'peace in our time' today, never mind expecting everyone to know where the phrase came from? Recent research into children's spirituality shows that children rapidly learn that spiritual experiences are not to be spoken of if they are to be taken seriously.[4] Our technological age does not have much room for transcendence for it prefers to control, manipulate and dominate the environment[5] (see Chapter 5).

The theologian David Tracy analysed negative or 'limit experiences', contrasting them with ecstatic experiences, which invite trust in a transcendent God.[6] Limit or negative experiences such as guilt, failure, anxiety, loneliness, sickness and death can either drive us towards God or push us away into unbelief. They may contain within them a signal of transcendence, such as a loving presence. Positive or ecstatic experiences such as joy, peace, creativity and love are signals of transcendence that invite the response of faith in the face of mystery. In his reading of the New Testament, Tracy argued that its diverse literary forms, which include parables, narratives, proverbs and eschatological sayings, correlate with the limit language and experiences of human beings. Tracy concluded that religious language is imaginative, analogical, mystical, metaphorical, mythical, symbolic and poetic. Such language 'disorientates us', redescribes our experience and 'discloses a limit referent which projects and promises that we can live a full and whole life in the presence of God who has made himself known in Christ'.[7] In spiritual direction we are trying to help people articulate their life story before God who is mystery – yet who is made known through self-revelation – by focusing on their spiritual experience. As they explore what is happening to them, the director helps them to understand their experience in the light of the life, death and resurrection of Jesus. Sometimes they may disclose experiences that make no sense to them whatsoever, and they may find it embarrassing to tell about these experiences or difficult to put them into words. It may well be that they have tried to do so already in their church setting and found rejection or mystification. Their experience may be very different from conventional religious experience. Spiritual direction may help them identify and then describe such moments.

Articulating mystery

There are many examples of mystery being described in textbooks on spiritual direction.[8] The person may be hesitant for fear of being misunderstood or laughed at. There may also be a sense of awe and wonder and perhaps gratitude for the experience. As a parish priest I frequently found myself doing spiritual direction on the hoof with people who hoped I could help them make sense of their spiritual experiences, good and bad: birth, death, beauty, the mysterious, things that made them feel small and insignificant or gave a glimpse of their uniqueness. It goes without saying that the reaction of directors to what they hear is crucial. For directees, the very act of learning to share their stories is an important part of growing in faith. As they do so they also learn to respond to their experience in the light of faith. While directors may desire to connect a directee's experience with the Christian story, it is important not to go too fast and impose religious imagery and language on another's articulated experience. Going slowly has the advantage of enabling directees to tease out their own experience of God, which may have taken place in an ordinary everyday setting rather than in prayer or during a 'contemplative moment'. They are thus better placed to realize that the whole of life may be filled with God's presence – in Elizabeth Barrett Browning's words: 'Earth's crammed with heaven, and every common bush afire with God; but only he who sees, takes off his shoes, the rest sit round it and pluck blackberries.'[9]

Whatever else we may say about the place of experience in the context of spiritual direction, it is experience that is going somewhere. It is interesting to note that many people who have had an experience of God in everyday life go on to participate in the Church's life because they notice a change in themselves when they do.

For directors who are listening, it is vital to know that we are being held in the great story as we listen to whoever is before us sharing theirs.

Spiritual direction and spiritual growth

When a person is baptized they are welcomed into the family of the Church, but that is not the end of the story – it is only the beginning of a lifelong spiritual journey towards God. Spiritual direction is usually entered into out of a desire to grow spiritually. My own experience of wanting something more is not an uncommon reason for people to seek out a spiritual director. It may not be felt in terms of a desire to grow but it represents a reaching out for something else beyond ourselves. There is a sense that there should be more to the Christian life than what we are currently experiencing, a desire to pray or a feeling that prayer is not all it could be. Issues are bound to arise as time goes by, but they are not the overriding motivation for receiving spiritual direction. By way of contrast, people usually enter into one of the available forms of therapy because of a particular issue or problem in their lives. They do so for a fixed period, even though this may last a number of years, as with psychotherapy. Growth may come about with stealth, slowly and almost imperceptibly, and that is how it is for most Christians. We are not the best people to comment on our own spiritual progress; it is others who notice the changes. As the mother of a teenager, however, I am aware that growth can also come about in fits and starts and sometimes in a huge spurt. It is often when someone is on the brink of a spiritual growth spurt that a spiritual director can be of real assistance, as well as during those long stretches of the humdrum and ordinariness of daily life.

The Bible and spiritual growth

Human lives have depth and texture and ideally we grow and develop not only physically but mentally and spiritually as well. In all the best literature there is depth and texture in the lives of the characters; in the Bible this is seen in the way they relate to God. The Bible narrates the progress of a people in a vividly human story of sin and repentance, wilderness and exile, conflict and struggle, all of which provides the stuff of spiritual direction. The illumination of the Spirit, the prophetic vision, the faithful and suffering servant fill the pages of the Old Testament and are relevant to every Christian seeking direction in the Way. In the New Testament we meet the culmination of

God's self-revelation in Jesus but we do not lose the idea of progress. We are exhorted to put our hand to the plough and not look back (Luke 9.62), to endure even to the end (Matt. 24.12–13), to run the race and prepare for the conflict (1 Cor. 9.24–26). There is a clear call to be fruitful and to press on towards the goal (Phil. 3.14–15) of maturity or spiritual adulthood.

It seems almost too obvious to state that if spiritual direction is about becoming more aware of God in every aspect of life and so growing in grace, the Bible, as God's self-revelation, is an indispensable tool. Yet many writers on spiritual direction do not make explicit reference to the Bible as the source of all directing.

If we wish to learn how to listen for God's word to us in the everyday, we need to examine closely how the living Word speaks to us in the written word. We should expect God to be consistent, which in turn gives us confidence when we detect divine presence and activity in our lives. Of course God is not shut up in a book – the Spirit who moved over the face of the waters in the beginning is ever present if we have eyes to see and ears to hear. Most of us, however, need constant reminders of the divine presence and activity around us and help in paying attention. The Bible is key to this process. It has always had a significant role in pastoral care in its broadest sense. Discussing the biblical nature of spiritual direction, Kenneth Leech stated: 'All theology is contemplative, a concentrated looking upon God as revealed in Christ, and manifested in lives which are hidden with Christ in God.'[10] Scripture shows us not only what this looks like but also how to set about it.

It may then come as a surprise that the Bible does not lay out a systematic plan for Christian discipleship. If it is a 'light to our path and a lamp to our feet', surely it should give us a set of clear instructions? It is not a manual for growth in that sense, however, for God created each one of us uniquely in God's own image and each one of us has to learn to relate to the Godhead out of who we are. Nevertheless, if we are learning to be followers of Jesus Christ it makes good sense to ask how the Lord himself lived his life. We have four accounts of his earthly life which, while not being straightforward biographies in the sense we understand that genre, tell us a great deal about the patterns and priorities he held during his life. Focusing on Jesus will help both director and directee remember what their relationship is based upon.

Using the Bible in spiritual direction will help raise our expectations that God is at work in us and will continue to be so. The spiritual director asks the question: 'Where has God been since we last talked?' And our reflections help us see that the same God who is at work in the Scriptures is also at work in us. We are then better placed to ask: 'Where will I meet God today?' and 'What is God going to do today?' Awareness of God in the ordinary moments of life will lead us back to the Scriptures and help us reflect on their meaning for us. Such awareness will help us to inhabit the Scriptures.

Inhabiting the Scriptures

Inhabiting or dwelling in the Scriptures is easily misunderstood. It does not mean using 'the language of Zion' in a quaint or artificial manner. We do not need to spout Bible verses or adopt 'Olde Englishe' speech. Indeed to do so would suggest the very opposite of inhabiting Scripture because it is so forced and unnatural. There will be meetings between two people for spiritual direction where the Bible is not mentioned explicitly at all, so what is going on? It would perhaps be better to think in terms of Scripture inhabiting us. As we feed on it, ruminating, digesting and internalizing its life-giving words, it begins to shape us, prompting our choices and decisions, guiding our pathways, correcting our attitudes and actions, comforting and strengthening us in new and unimagined ways. Familiarity will mean that some of it becomes logged in our memories and from there can influence our thinking. In 'Godly play' one of the phrases used frequently of characters in the Bible stories is 'Noah – for example – came so close to God and God came so close to him that he knew what God wanted him to do'.

Learning to inhabit the Scriptures is rather like learning a new language so that it becomes second nature. If we are to be really proficient at, say, French, we need to learn to think in French, maybe even dream in French. We reach the point where we can slip easily from one language to another without effort. We learn the idioms of speech of that language; its rules are embedded in our minds so that we do not need to pause to reach for the right mode of expression. Inhabiting the Scriptures is like this. It becomes second nature, or to use biblical language: our new nature.

A different metaphor that may help to illustrate what is intended is that of the sponge in the ocean. There it is floating freely and completely at home in its native environment. But is the ocean in the sponge or the sponge in the ocean? Has the living God made a home in me or am I at home in God? The presence and activity of the Holy Spirit in the business of holy listening is not in doubt. As Jesus himself promised in Matthew 18.20: 'For where two or three are gathered in my name, I am there among them.' Ideally both director and directee have separately and perhaps together invited the Holy Spirit to be present to lead us to the living Word.

The American pastor, writer and paraphraser of the Bible, Eugene Peterson, speaks of prayer as the language of the Christian Church where the Church is the language school and the Scriptures its textbook. Spiritual directors should perhaps be regarded as language assistants. When I was learning French at school we were guinea pigs for a brand new language laboratory. We sat in a booth and spoke into a microphone, having first listened via headphones to someone speaking to us in French. The language assistants, in some cases young French students, helped us interpret and form the words to sound more like a French speaker would pronounce them. So a spiritual director sits with us, listens with us and to us, and helps us to articulate what we are hearing and trying to respond to. There will be times when the spiritual director may need to press the pause button and ask directees what they mean by the religious word being used. Could they retranslate that word into plain everyday language? At other times the director may take the raw material of grace experienced and point the way to understanding where God is in it. To be able to do this interpretative task, directors will need to be paying attention to their own spiritual growth in which the Scriptures occupy a central place as the instrument of God's shaping of our lives into the likeness of Christ. They will be reading and meditating on God's word so that it nourishes them. They will remain open to its challenges as well as its comforts. They will speak to God about what they read and listen to the response of the Spirit speaking. In other words, they will need to be doing for themselves what they are seeking to help their directees to learn. Having one's own spiritual director and also receiving regular supervision is thus essential to be able to offer direction to others.

Learning to reflect theologically

Evagrius of Pontus (345–99) said that the one who prays is a theologian and a theologian is one who prays. Every Christian who begins to make connections with what they believe about God with the world around them and their everyday lives is doing theology. Reflecting is the simple exercise of thinking about the whys and wherefores of something, and we can reflect on anything. Theological reflection is concerned with faith seeking understanding. Like spiritual direction, it has become something of an industry in recent years – books about it pour off the presses. There are many similarities between the work of spiritual direction and theological reflection. In some ways all theological reflection is doing is helping to make explicit what all Christians do naturally; that is, to make connections by means of reflecting on life from God's point of view. It takes human experience and listens to it, taking it seriously in its own context while seeking to understand it from the standpoint of faith.

Experience for some Christians is problematic for it seems to undermine the authority of the word of God in Scripture. Arguably everything is experience. We come to the word of God via experience. We hear it read in church or we follow it in silence alone using our eyes and minds to absorb and understand it. How we are and what has been happening to us affects the way we hear and also our response. The writers of the Bible could only write what they experienced of God. The Psalms, for example, are the repository of every conceivable human emotion, over a third of which take the form of personal lament. The experience of life shaped what the ancient Israelites expressed to God and the form of that expression in turn shaped their experience.[11] In the New Testament we meet the apostle Paul who has taught us how to experience and talk about Christ. He could only say, 'I know the one in whom I have put my trust, and I am sure that he is able to guard until that day what I have entrusted to him' because he had experienced the truth of these words for himself (2 Tim. 1.12).

None of this is advocating a standpoint of self-absorption. What is being sought is self-awareness, which is very different because it has an outward as well as an inward dimension to it. Some of the most self-aware Christians in the history of the Church were the Desert Fathers and Mothers. They went into the desert in order to meditate on the Scriptures so that they could put them into practice in their desire to become holy like Christ himself. As they deepened their awareness of God's word, so they came to know themselves and their humanity. Holiness for them was all about interpreting Scripture and living it. They understood that interpreting Scripture necessitated practical action of the kind that leads to transformation. Their example is important for us here because of the importance they placed on spiritual direction and their influence on its subsequent history and development (see Chapter 7). The desert dwellers believed that discernment and self-knowledge were central to interpreting Scripture and that experience deepened interpretation and took them into new realms of spiritual growth and understanding. Prayer and Scripture mutually informed each other and faithful praxis led to growth in holiness.[12]

Another group of Christians, this time in sixteenth- and seventeenth-century England, collectively known as the Puritans, also focused their spirituality on the word of God, and they too came to have deep insight into the human condition. John Calvin opened his great work of theology with the words: 'Nearly all the wisdom we possess, that is to say, true and sound wisdom, consists of two parts: knowledge of God and of ourselves.'[13]

The theologian Nicholas Lash describes our relationship with the creed we profess in worship and praise as 'short words and endless learning'.[14] This could equally apply to the effect of meditating on short phrases from Scripture, returning to them again and again and finding ever fresh and deeper meaning in them. The Scriptures are food for the spiritual journey we are undertaking. It is up to us to make the connection between word and lived experience. Do we approach each day with the expectation that it is here that we will meet the God who speaks to us in God's word? Proverbs 6.22 shows how this can happen as we let God's word interact with our lives: 'When you walk, it will lead you; when you lie down, it will watch over you; and when you awake, it will talk with you.'

3

The Bible and spiritual direction

Were there spiritual directors in the Bible?

Bishop Kallistos Ware sees the ministry of the spiritual director as foreshadowed in the New Testament and quotes 1 Corinthians 4.15: 'For though you might have ten thousand guardians in Christ, you do not have many fathers. Indeed, in Christ Jesus I became your father through the Gospel.' Paul was an itinerant preacher rather than a director of souls, but there are some parallels worth consideration. Like a spiritual director, Paul felt a continuing responsibility for those whom he had led to faith in Christ, as well as an involvement with their struggles. He wrote to the Galatians with deep feeling: 'My little children, for whom I am again in the pain of childbirth until Christ is formed in you' (Gal. 4.19). Like the midwife or perhaps, here, the mother herself, he does not simply see them come to birth and then abandon them but continues to offer care as they begin to grow and develop. He shares their joys and sorrows as if they were his own: 'Who is weak, and I am not weak? Who is made to stumble, and I am not indignant?' (2 Cor. 11.29).

We could trace elements of spiritual direction even further back in the Old Testament – the Desert Fathers and Mothers certainly did so. The desert fathers and mothers were influenced by some of the words and images of the Old Testament also, especially Deuteronomy 32.7b: 'ask your father, and he will inform you; your elders, and they will tell you'. Today the concept of spiritual father, with its authoritarian connotations, may not be the best image of the spiritual director to use, though given the extent of lack of knowledge of the Bible in every way, the role that the abbas and ammas (see p. 74) played as wise and experienced guides may be one we need to recover. Antiquity was much better at recognizing the role of older people than our own society today, and while the Bible is not unequivocal in its praise of the elderly as wise guides, it is often the case that the old are given respect and in turn offer wise counsel. One thinks of Simeon and Anna, who watched and waited and whose patience enabled them to discern the Messiah when Mary and Joseph brought him into the temple. Simeon's song emerges out of a life soaked in Scripture and the expectation to which it gave rise.

There are other Old Testament precedents of spiritual guidance, however, in the prophets, priests and wise men and women – people like Moses, who spoke to God face to face and mediated between the people and God in the days when the Holy Spirit was restricted to individuals. As Jesus taught his disciples during his earthly life, he mediated his Father's wisdom to them directly: 'I have called you friends, because I have made known to you everything that I have heard from my Father' (John 15.15). Although at Pentecost the Holy Spirit fell on all the disciples, this does not seem to have dispensed with the need for wise counsel on the part of one mature Christian guiding a younger disciple, such as Paul instructing Timothy to 'Hold to the standard of sound teaching that you have heard from me, in the faith and love that are in Christ Jesus' (2 Tim. 1.13).

Throughout Christian history the Bible has played a key role in the way the Church has cared for and nurtured others. When we turn to the classic writings on prayer and spirituality we discover authors who write out of an atmosphere that lived and breathed the Scriptures. Augustine of Hippo, Bernard of Clairvaux, Julian of Norwich, Teresa of Ávila, John of the Cross, Martin Luther, John Calvin, George Herbert, John Bunyan, the Wesleys are just a few historical examples who might not continually quote the Bible directly but who took it for granted as the context out of which they lived. More recently, influential writers and spiritual leaders would include Brother Roger of Taizé, Henri Nouwen, Joyce Huggett, Gerard Hughes, Richard Foster, Dallas Willard and Eugene Peterson.[1]

Rooted and grounded in Scripture

The underlying premise of this book is that the Bible is indispensable for the ministry of spiritual direction. The question of how we read and interpret the Bible is, however, much contested. As spiritual direction has spread across different denominations and church traditions, this has become more of an issue than previously. Directors and directees may approach the Bible in very different ways, so there is a need for trust that each is free to use Scripture in their own way without seeking to impose this on the other.

Spiritual directors come from all Christian traditions and all desire good things for their directees. They long to see them flourish and to be able to find God in all of life. Most will have a regard for the Bible arising out of their own experience that sees it as playing an important part in the Christian life. They will be skilled at drawing from its riches in a variety of ways appropriate to the needs of the person before them. They will have an awareness of the way the Scriptures are viewed by different parts of the Church.

There is a perception of spiritual direction that seems to have more in common with psychotherapy than historical approaches to the practice of directing and which leaves little room for the place of Scripture as an authoritative source of spiritual growth. As our culture has lost confidence in the Christian narrative, the Church itself has felt undermined and suffered a loss of confidence in being distinctive. Spirituality is one of the most obvious signs of this loss of confidence as people who claim to be interested in spirituality reject the Church in the same breath. Spirituality, having been cut loose from its moorings, is all too often adrift. In its eagerness to appear non-partisan with something to offer all spiritual seekers, spiritual direction may be tempted to play down its origins in the Christian tradition, preferring to talk of God 'whoever God is for you' rather than the God of the Scriptures. Spiritual direction offered in this climate may seem little different from some of the other talking therapies on offer, with little to suggest that the Christian life is about transformation of our lives into the likeness of Christ. As someone remarked recently on checking out the content of a refresher course for spiritual directors, 'It sounds like alternative medicine.' God can be anything we want God to be, and the focus moves from God and God's designs for us to ourselves and our needs and desires. Rowan Williams has pointed out that 'without an anchorage in the word of God, we are insubstantial, distracted by our own private agendas and incapable of truthful relationship with each other.'[2] Knowing God and knowing ourselves go together, and Williams' comment is a reminder that we cannot know ourselves in isolation from other human beings either.

Spirituality and religion

While in theory the Church as a whole binds Christians together, in practice there is a growing divide between spirituality and formal religion. This situation has arisen for many reasons, and it affects church attenders as well as spiritual seekers who would not call themselves Christians.[3] If someone comes seeking direction who has been hurt by the Church in the past, spiritual directors may need to be very sensitive about the way they use Scripture, especially if it has played a part in the disillusionment of the person before them. Knowing how to support the many people who seek them out having given up on the Church is a big issue today for givers of spiritual direction. Indeed directors may themselves be among that disillusioned group of people. Spiritual direction may well be a lifeline for some who do not want to drift spiritually speaking but who have no intention of returning to the Church, at least at present. In the desire to support and encourage, spiritual directors may feel unable to use the very tool that has been part of the abuse or disillusionment and so the Scriptures are put to one side. It is helpful to be reminded of the historical nature of spiritual direction to set it in its original context of the believing community of faith, rooted in Scripture and serving the Church (see especially Chapter 7). To recognize where we are now and to catch a vision of where spiritual direction is going, we need to know where we have come from. Scripture itself insists we remember the rock from which we are hewn. When Joshua led the people of Israel over the River Jordan into the Promised Land, God told him to command them to set up 12 memory stones so that when the next generation came along and asked, 'What do these stones mean?' they could recount the story of where they had come from and what God had done (Josh. 1.1–7). There is great wisdom here for all who wonder at the cultural changes that are occurring both within and without the Church. When we feel the winds of change the temptation is to grasp the latest thing on offer, but the prophet Jeremiah urged the people to 'Stand at the crossroads, and look, and ask for the ancient paths, where the good way lies; and walk in it, and find rest for your souls' (Jer. 6.16). It is illuminating to note the comments of Kenneth Leech, who in many ways himself stood at the crossroads of change as spiritual direction was taking off for a new generation. Discussing the overlap between spiritual direction and psychotherapy in 1977, he insisted in the strongest terms that the ministry of the sacraments have a central role in spiritual direction. He stated:

> It is essential to stress this, for the individual who tries to exercise a ministry of personal guidance from the perimeters of the corporate Christian life is pursuing a course which is highly dangerous both to himself and to those who are subject to his influence.[4]

If this is true of the sacraments, it must also be true of the Scriptures.

Ten years later, the Revd Gordon Jeff wrote a slim volume called *Spiritual Direction for Every Christian* in which he expressed the conviction that every congregation included people who could and should be offering spiritual direction to others.[5] Not everyone would agree with his position, for spiritual direction still carries an air of an elitist pursuit for spiritual athletes or those who want to be seen to be taking their prayer seriously, rather like the person who in wanting to keep fit might employ a personal trainer today. There are those who shy away from seeing their skills in listening to others talk about their spiritual experiences because they do not feel qualified to take on such a responsible role. If we remember that this ministry is all about God and not about us, and that God has not left us alone to search in the dark, we do not need to be discouraged. With the current emphasis on the gifts of the Holy Spirit being given to the whole body of Christ for the upbuilding of that body, Jeff's stance is especially relevant. The Scriptures are full of unlikely people whom God has used to fulfil the divine purposes and bring blessing into the lives of others. With confidence in the Scriptures as God's reliable word, God's self-revelation and the Holy Spirit as our guide to understanding them, we are not left to random chance or our own fallible skills. This simple truth should give us confidence when we feel the weight of responsibility, and should also keep us humbly trusting when we are tempted to assume too much and work in our own strength.

Scripture and writers on spiritual direction

Few of the standard textbooks on spiritual direction refer explicitly to the place of the Scriptures in the ministry of directing. This is potentially a serious problem in today's spiritually confused climate.

Leech lamented the appalling ignorance of the Christian tradition among modern theologians, leading to 'current conventions' passing for orthodoxy and the most deeply rooted orthodox teachings being seen as a new discovery. He did not name ignorance of the Bible per se, but since most of the schools of prayer that have attained classic teaching on the subject are rooted in Scripture, his point reinforces Scripture's centrality at every moment in history to date. Whether we turn to East or West, to the anchorites of the Egyptian desert or the Wesley brothers in England, we will find that the Bible shapes and informs the patterns of spiritual guidance that are offered to ordinary Christians seeking help with their discipleship.

One recent book on spiritual direction to name the Bible explicitly as fundamental to the spiritual direction relationship is by the influential writer and spiritual guide Henri Nouwen. His book *Spiritual Direction*, compiled after his death, begins by outlining three classic disciplines or practices: look within to the heart; look to God in the book; look to others in community. The 'book' is the Bible, to which Nouwen insists we pay close attention as the word of God by devotional reading and meditating on the text. Meditation means 'eating the word, digesting it and incorporating it concretely into our lives'.[6] Regular attention to the Scriptures in this way will, over time, lead to the transformation of our personal identity, our actions and our common life of faith. We do not simply seek to be instructed or informed, Nouwen notes, but formed. The book quotes, alludes, refers and is constructed around biblical models of spiritual formation designed to aid those seeking God.

Margaret Guenther's book *Holy Listening* is saturated with Scripture.[7] Its three fundamental models of directing – teacher, midwife and giver of hospitality – are all rooted in biblical stories and metaphors, and Guenther explores these fully in refreshing and original ways (see Chapter 7).

One final example of writing on spiritual direction that highlights the place of the Bible is a psychological approach to the ministry of spiritual direction, Chester P. Michael's *An Introduction to Spiritual Direction*.[8] Although Michael's book is based on the course he teaches during a two-year programme for spiritual directors that is based on the depth psychology of Carl Jung, he grounds his aims and understanding of what spiritual direction is for in the biblical narratives going back to Moses in the desert. Admittedly Michael has a wide definition of what constitutes spiritual direction, but he locates himself firmly within the Christian tradition and makes frequent reference to the Bible. In listing 25 purposes of spiritual direction, however, learning how to use the Bible in prayer and personalizing the word of God comes in at number 21.

Life-giving words

Christians believe that God's written word testifies to the living Word, the Lord Jesus Christ.

> Blessed be the God and Father of our Lord Jesus Christ . . . With all wisdom and insight he has made known to us the mystery of his will, according to his good pleasure that he set forth in Christ, as a plan for the fullness of time, to gather up all things in him, things in heaven and things on earth.   (Eph. 1.3, 8–10)

As directors and directees approach the Scriptures, they can be assured they are handling God's word to us that is personal and life giving. While directors may need to take the lead and model that assurance in their personal stance, both need to know they cannot control the Scriptures. These have a life of their own. The Bible's authority goes beyond the question of its accuracy. When we trust that they are the word of God to us they become the word of life to us (John 6.68), words that encompass all that is because they emanate from the God who is immense and other and yet closer to us than our own breath. Sitting under Scripture is perhaps not enough. As the image of the sponge in the ocean described above, we need to be immersed in Scripture, to learn to inhabit it so that it becomes home ground, familiar territory, somewhere we can move freely and know we are at home. There is a sense in which the Scriptures offer us the hospitality of God. In Isaiah 55 the prophet proclaims God's invitation to the abundant life: 'Ho, everyone who thirsts, come to the waters; and you that have no money, come, buy and eat! Come, buy wine and milk without money and without price' (Isa. 55.1). The section ends with a picture of people moving about freely and safely: 'For you shall go out in joy, and be led back in peace' (v. 12). Connected with this picture of harmony is God's word:

> For as the rain and the snow come down from heaven, and do not
> return there until they have watered the earth, making it bring forth
> and sprout, giving seed to the sower and bread to the eater, so shall
> my word be that goes out from my mouth; it shall not return to me
> empty, but it shall accomplish that which I purpose.   (vv. 10–11)

It follows that spiritual directors must be confident that the Scriptures
are the word of God for themselves as well as for others. They need
to be able to listen to them in faith and offer them in hope and love
to others so that they may learn to listen also. The best training
spiritual directors can have in preparation for their art is to pay
attention to how God is working in their own lives and to deepen
their own experience of God through the word. If the Bible is the
basic tool of spiritual directors, it is vital that we use it regularly
ourselves and are confident in handling it. We need to be open to
hearing God speak to us through its words before we can facilitate
others in listening. If this seems too great a burden to bear, we need
to remember that it is Jesus, who is the fulfilment of all the law and
the prophets, who interprets the Scriptures to us (Heb. 1.1–2). We
do not need to be anxious that it all depends on us. In his letter to
the Thessalonians Paul wrote:

> We also constantly give thanks to God for this, that when you received
> the word of God that you heard from us, you accepted it not as a
> human word but as what it really is, God's word, which is also at work
> in you believers.   (1 Thess. 2.13)

The Holy Spirit and spiritual direction

If the Holy Spirit is the true director we may be sure that even though
our words are spoken at a human level, it is God who will open the
hearts of others to hear the living Word. We are the human instru-
ments through which the Spirit works. Words matter, but the word
God speaks to us is in a different category from the words we use to
communicate information or give commands. God's word in the
Bible is

> intended, whether confrontationally or obliquely, to get inside us, to
> deal with our souls, to form a life that is congruent with the world
> that God has created, the salvation that he has enacted and the com-
> munity that he has gathered.[9]

It is the Holy Spirit who brings the word alive and makes it effectual. It is the Holy Spirit who works in the human heart to open it to hear God's word, to tune in to the divine voice speaking through its pages and to respond in faith and trust. The Holy Spirit's part in the ministry of spiritual direction is crucial first of all because the Spirit is crucial to the life of every believer.

In John 14.23–26 Jesus said:

> Those who love me will keep my word, and my Father will love them, and we will come to them and make our home with them. Whoever does not love me does not keep my words; and the word that you hear is not mine, but is from the Father who sent me. I have said these things to you while I am still with you. But the Advocate, the Holy Spirit, whom the Father will send in my name, will teach you everything, and remind you of all that I have said to you.

The Holy Spirit, the real spiritual director, is our teacher and also the key to our memory. It is the Spirit who teaches us about Jesus whom we follow and whose likeness is growing in us; the same Spirit also reminds us of what Jesus has said. There is more to say about memory and the need to recover our ability to store up treasure within. The Spirit explains and instructs and brings to mind those things we need to remember at the appropriate moment. The Spirit is at work in us, making it possible for us to hear God speaking to us, helping us to understand and giving us the power to apply what we hear to our lives. This is going on at all times and not just during spiritual direction of course – an important truth to bear in mind.

There are other points to notice in this important passage in John 14 that are central to spiritual direction. Jesus himself comes to us and makes his home in us. We are seeking to know him and he is here, with us now, graciously accepting the hospitality of our hearts. In turn he invites us to make our home in him, to dwell in his word (the Jerusalem Bible translates another verse, John 8.31, as 'if you make my word your home'). This promise of intimacy with Jesus is for all believers and is the foundation on which our growth as followers who are being made more like him is based. If we have confidence in Jesus we may have confidence in his word to us too. And here he makes it clear that the words he speaks to us are the Father's words as well as his.

In Ephesians 1.13–18 Paul sets out God's great eternal design for creation.

> In him you also, when you had heard the word of truth, the gospel of your salvation, and had believed in him, were marked with the seal of the promised Holy Spirit; this is the pledge of our inheritance towards redemption as God's own people, to the praise of his glory. I have heard of your faith in the Lord Jesus and your love towards all the saints, and for this reason I do not cease to give thanks for you as I remember you in my prayers. I pray that the God of our Lord Jesus Christ, the Father of glory, may give you a spirit of wisdom and revelation as you come to know him, so that, with the eyes of your heart enlightened, you may know what is the hope to which he has called you.

Paul is pointing out that the Ephesian Christians had not simply heard the word of truth but they had believed also. They were thus sealed with the Holy Spirit who had been promised and who is 'the pledge of our inheritance' now until we gain full possession. And all for the glory of God. It is the Spirit who guides us and enlightens our minds and gives us hope. This is the same Spirit who searches the depths of God (Rom. 8), who searches our hearts. When we pray we do so in collaboration with the Holy Spirit (Phil. 1.19).

The Bible, spiritual direction and the Church

As we connect with God's word we are also connecting with the whole Church, past and present, whose countless believers have heard and obeyed and are doing so along with us today. Here we are reminded again of how important it is to remain connected with the wider Church and how spiritual direction helps us to do that as we listen with another to God speaking to us in God's unique way for our lives. When the Bible is read in Church it is shaping the minds and hearts of the worshippers present. It orders the Church's life and energizes it for mission. Spiritual direction takes up its task within this framework. Preachers also have a role as they expound the word of God in church, which helps directors and directees grow in understanding since both belong to a learning community of faith, albeit in different places. The word of God as the source of nourishment for Christians is complemented by the sacraments of the Church, especially regular participation in Holy Communion. The one is never meant to replace the other, rather each should strengthen the value of the other and illuminate their importance in the lives of every Christian.

For many people today, including Christians in the Church, the Bible is a disconnected set of writings they have encountered in different ways. They may have learned the ten commandments, the Lord's Prayer and Psalm 23 as children if they are pre-generation Y. They may have favourite passages they turn to from time to time. They may not have any sense, however, of the unity of the Bible with its overarching story. The Bible claims to tell the true story of the world and its meaning. It begins with the creation of the world and runs right through the history of Israel to Jesus. It does not stop there but continues on to look forward to the coming of the kingdom of God in all its fullness. Jesus Christ is at the centre of the whole story and the Bible claims that in him has been revealed God's fullest purpose and meaning for the world. It is only as we grasp this and learn to live in this story that we will find not only the meaning of the world but the meaning of our own lives as well. This is not easy to hear in a postmodern world that claims to have rejected all over-arching stories. But the Bible has to be taken on its own terms if it is to shape the lives of those who come to it seeking the way to live.

Alasdair MacIntyre tells an amusing story to make the point that we all depend on some kind of story to make sense of our lives. He imagines he is at a bus stop when a young man standing next to him suddenly says: 'The name of the common wild duck is histrionicus, histrionicus, histrionicus.' Although we understand the meaning of the sentence, why would he say that? It can only be understood if we know the wider context, the story in the background that gives it a broader framework of meaning. Three possible stories lend themselves to the scenario. First, the young man could have mistaken the man standing next to him for someone else he met at the library yesterday who asked him if he knew the Latin name of the common duck. Or he could have just come from seeing his psychotherapist who is helping him to deal with his painful shyness. The therapist urged him to talk to strangers. When the young man said 'What shall I say?' The therapist responded 'Anything.' Third, he could be a spy who has arranged to meet his contact at this bus stop. The code that will identify him is the statement about the Latin name of the common duck. The meaning of the encounter at the bus stop is dependent on which story is shaping it, and each story related here will give it a different meaning.[10]

There have been a number of attempts by the Christian Church to help people engage with the Scriptures in creative ways, some of which have been aimed at believers and others more widely. Bible studies and commentaries continue to be produced; these deal with detail and are mainly cerebral in approach. Bible Society has initiated a number of projects aiming to raise the profile of the Bible in the wider culture. Meanwhile the Bible Reading Fellowship has launched a new approach to spending time with God in the Scriptures through *Quiet Spaces*, published three times a year. This self-consciously offers a different methodology, designed to help people come to Scripture in more imaginative ways, and offers a variety of approaches in each booklet. It also eschews dates so that people can work at their own pace and in whatever timescale they wish.

'The Big Read' was a venture designed to get the whole Bible read aloud by many voices in one go. It co-opted a number of well-known faces in the media to take part alongside anyone who wanted to join in with reading a section. 'Walk-thru the Bible' is another project designed to be used in churches and schools to give an overview of the big picture of what the Bible is all about.[11] For Christian readers the choice of books about the Bible is huge, and they cover every flavour on the spectrum of the Church. The same is true of books on prayer – there is seemingly no shortage of interest here either. But as many people know, reading books about something and participating in courses and projects is not the same as engaging in it oneself. There is a story from the desert about two brothers who came to an old man at Scetis and announced their proficiency with the Bible. One of them proclaimed: 'I have learned the Old and New Testaments by heart.' The old man responded: 'You have filled the air with words.' So where does spiritual direction fit into this world that is searching for a story to live by?

The anchor of the Scriptures

At present spiritual directors are not accredited. Unlike counsellors who undergo rigorous training and have to be registered in order to practise, spiritual direction is still seen as an informal ministry – good directors often known through word of mouth. In effect anyone who chooses can put a plaque on their door saying 'Spiritual director' and offer their services. Some charge a fee, others do not, and feelings run high on both sides of the divide. Many who offer direction are clergy or religious, and these are to some extent accountable because of their particular status. But increasingly lay people, often having done some sort of training, are also offering direction. Most will have had some kind of vetting and their names will be on a list held by a diocese or one of the spirituality networks that exist. As with counselling, all spiritual directors who provide direction for others will have their own spiritual director. In addition, supervision is increasingly sought, and there is a growing body of trained supervisors. Others opt for peer supervision. There are courses and refresher training days in almost all parts of the UK.

Given this situation there are inevitably calls for more vetting of spiritual directors and more control over who may practise. It is one very important reason why this ministry needs to be seen as operating out of the Christian Church and on behalf of the Church. It takes us back to the question of what spiritual direction is for and what is its relation to the body of Christ. It is a corporate not an individualistic enterprise. Keeping the Scriptures at the heart of direction is one way of ensuring that spiritual direction does not come adrift from its moorings within the Church and end up simply encouraging people to make up a spirituality of their own to suit their own desires. The wisdom that the spiritual director exercises derives from the Christian community as a whole and is for the upbuilding of that community. In his classic book on community, *Life Together*, Dietrich Bonhoeffer wrote:

> God has willed that we should seek and find his living Word in the witness of a brother, in the mouth of man. Therefore the Christian needs another Christian who speaks God's Word to him. He needs him again and again when he becomes uncertain and discouraged, for by himself he cannot help himself without belying the truth.[12]

The New Testament makes continual reference to the value of having others to encourage, support and guide us in our Christian lives: 'love one another with mutual affection; outdo one another in showing honour' (Rom. 12.10); 'instruct one another' (Rom 15.14); 'be kind to one another . . . forgiving one another' (Eph. 4.32); 'Bear one another's burdens' (Gal. 6.2).

Interpreting the Bible

How is Scripture authoritative for Christians? In what way is it? To what end? With what claim? As God's word it carries authority for all Christian believers, but it is a well-known fact that they frequently disagree as to its meaning. God's word is not a set of propositions but a richly varied collection of different genres that require us to be open to their truth in challenging and transformative ways. Walter Brueggemann states: 'Obedient communities of faith are the proper venue for Scripture interpretation, even though they may be well informed by the critics' study that is offered by the academy.'[13] Anyone entrusted with interpreting Scripture – and here I would include spiritual directors in this awesome task – has both a weighty responsibility to decide what the text may be saying and at the same time great freedom in that act of interpretation. As a result, the act of interpretation involves 'making' meaning as well as 'finding' it. Interpretation thus becomes 'an imaginative act of reconstruction', where imaginative does not signify free rein to make it mean whatever we choose.[14]

Interpretation of Scripture is unavoidable, and as Brueggemann points out, interpretation is always advocacy about which there is dispute.[15] We are not only talking about the exegesis of the text but which translation we choose; why this text and not that one in this situation. Even the tone and inflection of voice when we read the Bible in public involves an interpretative act. Interpretation is always mediated through the voice, hopes, perceptions, fears, interests and hurts of the interpreter and of the context of interpretation. Since interpretation is never wholly objective, it must always be partial and provisional. This is why the whole Church must be involved in interpreting its book and not collude with an individualistic culture that tries to make it a matter of private concern. God's word to us is always personal, but never private.

How do we read the Bible devotionally?

Reading the Bible devotionally is not an alternative to applying our minds and the accumulated scholarship of generations of Bible students who have wrestled with its meaning; but unless we hear the word of God as addressed to us personally, we will have missed the

point of the written word. In approaching the Scriptures devotionally we are seeking to bring words together rather than taking
them apart. The point is not to wonder whether we agree with them
or not but to hear them speaking to us in our situation as God's
personal word to us. They are words that are meant to get from our
heads deep down into the innermost parts of our being, penetrating
every corner of our hearts until we are transformed by them.

The Bible is not one book but a whole body of literature covering
many centuries. It needs to be approached with expansive hearts and
minds that ache to hear God's word for today. Of course, we can be
theologically literate but still miss the point. Nicodemus, a teacher
of spiritual things, was nevertheless unable to understand what Jesus
was saying to him about spiritual growth when they met by night to
talk (John 3.1–21).

The Bible has been a resource for living and a guide to what to do
next for countless Christians down the centuries. It is God's word to
us and in very direct and arresting ways. It is a resource for living
and will often show us the way to go, but there is much more to say
besides and many qualifications along the way. The Bible is not just
a book about 'Jesus and me'; interpreting Scripture is never a purely
private enterprise. For example, the God of personal salvation is
also the God of the nations who demands justice. When Christians
doggedly refuse to imagine that God's anger at injustice and oppres-
sion expressed in Scripture has anything to do with us, we too have
misunderstood the God of the Bible. The same Christians who get
hot under the collar regarding sexual ethics, for example, may be less
disposed to take seriously what Jesus said about, say, wealth. We all
have blind spots and need help in discerning where these lie.

There remains the imperative need to let the word of God dwell
richly in us so that it addresses us personally in our hearts. It has to
become the centre of our being and the wellspring of our actions.
The Bible does speak personally to us yet never submits to our whims
or our needs.

Spiritual directors can draw on the scholarship of commentators
who have studied the original context of Scripture and worked at what
it meant in its own time. This is important but it is not the whole
story. What it means today, to me and to the Church, is also fundamental to the way God speaks. This is where biblical interpretation
needs imagination as well as careful and detailed textual study. The

Holy Spirit still 'blows where it chooses' (John 3.8) and brings the Scriptures to life in endless new contexts. Spiritual direction is not designed to replace Bible study, but it insists that God continues to speak personally to people who have ears to hear. Like the Desert Fathers and Mothers, we are less concerned with theological debate than with practical application where spiritual direction is concerned.

In Matthew 7.28–29 Jesus spoke 'as one having authority, and not as their scribes'. Those who listened to Jesus heard a different kind of voice: they could hear God speaking to them. Read the whole 'Sermon on the Mount' and hear challenge but also encouragement. There is a sense of God's closeness to us, God's approachability and tenderness (see also Luke 4.16–22). Hearing Jesus teach in this way is a reminder of the difference between academic study of Scripture and hearing it as the power of God to transform us. Even in the difficult times, Jesus comes to us with compassion and offers strength and healing as well as guidance and direction (see Matt. 9.35–36; 11.28–30).

Alongside personal Bible study and the public and communal reading of Scripture, Christians turn to the Bible to hear what God is saying to us as individuals, and spiritual direction is unashamedly seeking to discern what God is saying to me in the midst of my daily experience. The Scriptures have always been read devotionally by all Christian traditions with the expectation that God will guide, comfort, challenge and tell us what we need to hear. But it is a mistake to think that using the Bible devotionally lets us off learning how to read Scripture wisely and responsibly. We are not to suppose that the Bible is some kind of lucky dip or Christian version of a horoscope. God wants us to hear the divine voice, and Scripture is one of the most important ways the word speaks to us. As we learn to recognize God's voice in its pages we will grow in our awareness of the Lord speaking at other times too. I am a keen bird watcher and believe firmly that God speaks to me through these wonderful and diverse creatures. Every sparrow that pecks at the crumbs on the bird table reminds me that God cares for me (see Matt. 10.29–31). Do I need to know the Bible verse that tells me that not a single sparrow falls to the ground without my heavenly Father knowing? No, I do not, but how much richer that tender image becomes when I listen to Jesus telling me that not a single sparrow falls to the ground without my heavenly father – and his – knowing. Certainly, knowledge of that verse enriches my understanding, while the simplicity of an ordinary bird in my garden causes me to wonder. The joy of it is that I may also be drawn to Scripture to deepen and confirm the instinct that there is a creator God who rejoices in the detail of this most amazing world. God speaks in all kinds of ways, not least through creation and through the circumstances of our lives. It is when all these come together that we can begin to learn to live deeply and with so much more awareness. We need to be careful all the same, not to confuse devotion with authority. It is easy to get it wrong, and the temptation to put 'God told me' at the start of a sentence has led to a great deal of self-deceit and destruction. As N. T. Wright argues, the role of Scripture in the life of the Church and of the individual Christian indicates three things.[16] First that God speaks, God communicates in words. Second that God's words are instrumental in bringing about transformation of the kind that makes us more like Jesus Christ. This of course is the work in which spiritual direction is a tool. Romans 12 exhorts us to 'be transformed by the renewing of your minds' (v. 2). We are to think in new ways. Words are intrinsic to how we think, so it is unsurprising that words in a book are central to this. Third, the Scriptures show us how God's purpose is focused on transforming not only individual lives but the whole world. They help us to understand and play our part in joining in with what God is doing, for as we shall see, spiritual direction, like the Scriptures that inform this ministry, is about sending us back into the world to live out our calling as human beings made in God's image.

Listening to the Scriptures

It will be clear by now that listening is central to the art of spiritual direction. In prayer we are bold enough to approach a God who listens to us with loving attention, and in spiritual direction we are seeking to listen with discerning ears. Spiritual directors are practising double listening – to God and to the person before them. This may be the only occasion this person is genuinely listened to, which in itself is a profoundly valuable gift to give another human being. If we do not have the experience of being listened to, it will be harder to practise listening ourselves and also harder to express what is going on inside. To realize that God listens to us is the first step in desiring the Spirit to speak to us in turn and so begin the process of learning to recognize the divine voice. God is always speaking to us if only we can tune in. We need to listen with our eyes as well as our ears; indeed listening involves the whole of our being as we sift and sort and practise hearing the voice of the Lord, which sometimes whispers and at other times thunders to us (1 Kings 19). We are learning to see the world through God's eyes, to hear God's voice and to recognize God's ways deep within our spirits. Margaret Guenther regards the spiritual director as both a learner and a teacher of discernment, and the latter as a two-stage process.[17] First there is perception: 'Where is God in this?' and second there is right judgement: 'What to do with this perception of God?' Thus directors have to be able to practise discernment towards directees but equally importantly must help them develop their own ability to discern for themselves.

How do we do all this deep listening? The word 'habitus' describes a way of living that is immersed in the Christian faith, from which comes a disposition of mind and heart and from which our actions flow. It is a practical knowing that has the primary character of wisdom.[18] It grows as we immerse ourselves in the lived experience of faith, which includes regular patterns of reading Scripture and joining in a worshipping community. In other words it is about 'life in the Spirit'. Naturally we resist this. As Paul knew so well (see Romans 7), the 'old' character of every human being kicks back against the 'new' person in Christ. It requires all of us: our minds and hearts, our imaginations and wills, our souls and bodies, our prayers and our obedience. Where Scripture is concerned, developing a habitus means receiving the words deep into us so that they form us. They become interior to our lives such that we inhabit them as they inhabit us. The Latin word for 'obedience', *ob-audire*, contains the verb 'to listen', for the two are closely connected. The words of Scripture become part of our vocabulary and so do the rhythms and images of Scripture, so that they flow out of us in prayer and loving acts. This is where the image of eating the Bible may be helpful, for as the food we chew and digest becomes our tissue and muscles and issues forth in energy, so the words of the Bible become part and parcel of who we are and how we are in the world. When I was visiting the Cape of Good Hope we called in on a museum en route. It had many stuffed animals, some behind glass. They were interesting and we could look at our leisure and take in the detail. But when we went outside and saw other animals in their natural habitat, living and breathing, walking and running free, how alive they were, how beyond our grasp, and a joy to behold! That is what it means to experience the Scriptures as words of life rather than dead letters on a page.

Scripture in performance

Jesus often seems to have taught on the move. A large section of Luke's Gospel, for example, is known as the Travelogue because Jesus teaches and heals as he journeys on. This is a helpful reminder that we do not necessarily have to be in church or even settled into a private time of prayer for God to break into our lives with a nudge, a whisper or indeed a shout. God speaks to us in and through our ordinary lives. That is why Scripture is full of rural imagery, for that is what was familiar to everyone in both the Old and the New Testaments – gardens, farming, landscapes, birds and trees, to name just a few. Jesus used ordinary everyday things to teach people about the kingdom of God, but he explained to his disciples that only those with eyes to see and ears to hear would understand. Without this gift of discernment people simply heard stories of everyday things: farmers sowing seed, merchants seeking pearls, a woman sweeping a room. Although Matthew features the Sermon on the Mount, Luke located Jesus' first sermon on the plain (Luke 6.17–20), suggesting that Jesus is content to get involved in our lives at our level in the pressure of everyday life. The people brought their needs to him: sickness, troubled minds and so on. Jesus cared about the things they were concerned with. In spiritual direction nothing is beyond the realms of legitimate attention, and the conversation is more likely than not to centre on something that happened in an ordinary setting. In *The Voyage of the Dawn Treader*, one of the Chronicles of Narnia by C. S. Lewis, Lucy found an ancient book in which she found a spell to make Aslan the lion visible, though he had to inform her that he had been present all the time.[19]

So what does it mean to reflect on the Bible in the light of my experience of life in all its dimensions? The metaphor sometimes used is that of performance. Whether it is a piece of music or a part in a play, the idea of performing the Scriptures is a helpful one in connection with the content of spiritual direction. Like music, the Bible comes alive as we learn to live it out. A piece of music that remains written on the page but never performed is never heard. Can it really be called music? The musician picks up the page and plays and thus performs the music. It is important to reproduce the notes accurately but that is not all there is to it, at least not in a virtuoso performance. Listening to a pianist like Murray Perahia play Bach's *Goldberg Variations* is to hear all the notes played accurately but with life and energy and understanding that can interpret the inner meaning of the notes on the stave. He does not add anything or leave anything out, but his performance has enabled his own self to become part of the life of the piece. Perhaps spiritual direction should be thought of as a duet where director and directee listen to one another in order to hear the music of the Spirit and respond together to its tune.

Another analogy in a similar vein is the way a play works. One actor gives a performance of *Hamlet* that is electrifying but then we see the play again and a different actor brings out new dimensions that we had not seen before. Both speak the words as they stand in the script, both give excellent performances, but they are alive and unique. Music and drama have to be 'realized' in performance, and so it is with Scripture. The reflection on the way that Scripture and life come together and what the Holy Spirit is doing in the midst of it all is the stuff of spiritual direction.[20] In *The Voyage of the Dawn Treader*, Lucy discovered that as she turned the pages of the ancient book, she unconsciously grew more and more beautiful. Such is the power of God in the Scriptures to transform lives so that they reflect his nature.

4

The use and abuse of the Bible in spiritual direction

————◆·◆·◆————

There was a time when abusing the Bible meant damaging its physical contents, and school children who have been introduced to Robert Louis Stevenson's *Treasure Island* will all remember the black spot on the torn page of Scripture. But there is more than one way to abuse the written word of God, and the resulting damage may be immense and lasting.

There were instances in the desert when a fundamental misunderstanding of the text of Scripture and its role in human lives prevented would-be disciples not only from practising it but also from fulfilling the spirit of the word. In one such story a brother who went to seek counsel from Abba Silvanus noticed the brothers who were with him working hard. He quoted the Bible to Silvanus: 'Do not work for the food that perishes' (John 6.27) and 'Mary has chosen the better part' (Luke 10.42). Silvanus responded by having one of his disciples give the seeker a book and take him to his cell, where he could get on with his reading. When the ninth hour came the visitor expected to be called for a meal but nothing happened. He went to Silvanus and asked: 'Have the brothers not eaten today?' The old man replied that they had. 'Why did you not call me?' Silvanus replied 'Because you are a spiritual man and do not need that kind of food. We, being carnal, want to eat and that is why we work. But you have chosen the good portion and read the whole day long and you do not want to eat carnal food.' When he heard Silvanus' reply the visitor prostrated himself and said: 'Forgive me, Abba.' Silvanus said: 'Mary needs Martha. It is really thanks to Martha that Mary is praised.'[1]

As in many stories that display the wisdom of the desert, this tale shows how the elders were able to show in a practical and also an

43

ironical way what a particular text meant and what it might mean to fulfil it. They were thus able to take others with them and lead them into the world of the Scriptures themselves so that they too could begin to inhabit it. Here Silvanus showed his visitor what it meant to bring the text to life and in doing so showed him a way of life that is whole.

A dualistic approach to spirituality is only one way that the Bible may be applied in an unhelpful way.

Bible heroes?

Learning about people in the Bible who prayed and who seemed to know God so intimately could lead us to conclude that the characters of the Scriptures are very different from us. We are not great evangelists like Paul, prayer warriors like Nehemiah, obedient like Mary or people of faith like Abraham. Many people have been taught to see these heroes and heroines of the faith as exactly that: men and women to learn from and emulate, with the expectation that we will be just like them. Certainly we should expect that God wants the same kind of intimacy with us that is apparent in the Bible, but we need to be realistic about such men and women rather than placing them on pedestals that tower over our heads. Using Bible characters whom we have turned into super-saints to beat ourselves up with is not a helpful way into reflecting on their relationships with God and what they may teach us.

Damaged people

The current climate of dissatisfaction with the institutional Church presents a dilemma for spiritual directors. Often the people who come to us are people who have been damaged by the Church in some way or other. They may be deeply hurt, disillusioned, even angry at their treatment at the hands of other Christians. Such treatment may have included unhelpful readings of the Bible.

In John 6.67 Jesus asked the disciples if they were going to abandon him like the rest, and Philip replied, 'Lord, to whom can we go? You have the words of eternal life' (v. 68). The Bible contains words of life that have been variously described as honey to the taste, life-giving streams of water, food for the soul and a light to our path, to name a few of the many rich metaphors. How is it, then, that so often we manage to turn these words of life into words of death and destruction? How have we altered what writers have described as God's love letter to us to make it a book of rules and regulations that we have no hope of keeping? Too many people have rejected what they think is the word of God because it has been handed out to them in poor, shallow and rigid ways. In such a climate, spiritual directors may find themselves having to undo large amounts of misinformation before they can turn to the Scriptures as healing balm and music for confused and world-weary ears. So it must be acknowledged that while the Bible plays a central role in the work of directing, applying it wisely is not automatically straightforward.

What the Bible is not

Using the Bible to coerce, browbeat or condemn someone is counter-productive and contrary to what the word of God is about. It is almost as important to say what the Bible is not as it is to set out what it is. The Bible is not a textbook of pronouncements that we apply in a two-dimensional way to our lives. Nor is it a blueprint of what a Christian should look like. Nor again is it a mysterious code that yields the key to existence to those who manage to crack it. There is a grain of truth in each of these caricatures, but taking them at face value will not help people wanting more from their relationship with God any more than they will enable a spiritual director to work well with others. Spiritual directors are not in the business of pronouncing Bible texts over people, though they may cite it frequently and offer texts for prayer and meditation. Nor are they trying to clone people to fit some kind of preconceived individual template. They are certainly not the guardians of a mysterious body of knowledge or the key that unlocks the Bible code for people. In many parish churches of the post-Reformation period huge boards were erected on which were inscribed the ten commandments, Lord's Prayer and the Apostles' Creed. In one sense we might think that such focus on God's word merits approval, until we recall that this same period dubbed the Church of England 'high and dry'. Words of life had been fossilized and were little more than a means of moralizing. In the Victorian period many homes had the text from Genesis 16.13, 'Thou God see-est me' over the mantelpiece (*El-roi*: 'God of seeing' or 'God who sees' – NRSV footnote). They are wonderful words uttered by Abraham's maltreated slave Hagar and are echoed in Psalm 139 and elaborated on there, but the Victorians understood them as belonging to a God who never missed anything we did wrong and who was always waiting to pounce. Our image of God will dictate how we read God's messages to us.

The Bible and spiritual directors

When I began my curacy as a single woman, my training incumbent advised me to work out how I felt about marriage and about conducting marriage services; for, he warned, if I was uncomfortable, it would show. It was wise counsel and it applies here to spiritual directors and the Scriptures.

It goes without saying that spiritual directors in the Christian tradition will have some idea of what it means to be a Christian. It is unlikely, however, that they will present themselves as experts in prayer, for none of us feels competent in this. It is far more likely they will describe themselves as fellow seekers. They will have a relationship with God as made known in Christ and they will be seeking to grow in that relationship themselves. They will have some skill in handling the tools of direction that will include different ways of appropriating the Scriptures in prayer. Any director to whom the Bible is a closed book will be unlikely to place a high value on it as a guide to the spiritual life.

One of the most influential spiritual directors in the Anglican tradition during the early part of the twentieth century was the laywoman Evelyn Underhill. Her spiritual director was another important figure at this time, Friedrich von Hügel. In describing how he had helped her to pray she wrote:

> When I went to the Baron [von Hügel] he said I wasn't much better than a Unitarian. Somehow by his prayers or something, he compelled me to experience Christ. He never said anything more about it – but I know, humanly speaking, he did it. It took about four months – it was like watching the sun rise very slowly – and then suddenly one knew what it was . . . I seem now to try as it were to live more and more towards him only . . . The New Testament . . . now seems full of things never noticed – all gets more and more alive and compellingly beautiful.[2]

It has been repeatedly stated that awareness is key to the whole direction process. Awareness of God at all times is the goal of spiritual direction. It also needs to be to the fore during direction.

Both directors and directees work out of operative as well as espoused theologies. It is vital as directors that we are aware of our operative theology and are working towards congruency with our espoused theology.

There may be some tension between an expectation that, as in counselling, spiritual directors should work with unconditional acceptance of the theology of their directees, and a desire to enable directees to experience more of the grace of God in Christ. Directors also work from their own theologies of religious experience and grace and need constant vigilance against the unconscious desire to create directees in their own image. They need to recognize that they may be working from a different theology from the person before them. Occasionally when someone asks me to help them find a spiritual director they will specify that the person should be from a particular tradition. While I always explain that a good director will be open to people of all traditions, there may be good reason for caution on the part of someone who has been told their theology is wrong by a person in authority.

As directees narrate life events since their last meeting, directors will be listening carefully. They will ask, 'Where is God in all this?' and continue to ask appropriate questions as directees try to make sense of their experience. This is the work of interpretation, and it is delicate work. We are treading on holy ground. It is crucial at this point that directors should not say what this or that experience 'means' nor be too quick to impose a passage of Scripture on it and so close down the discussion. Telling directees that such and such an experience is like something in the Bible may feel restricting or be so authoritative that there is no room to reject or query it. Directees may stop exploring at this point, feeling that the right 'answer' has been found.

Text and context

Many people today have no language to describe faith. It is not just that they do not know the stories of the Bible (who Abraham, Moses and so on were or what they did), but that they may never have come across words like 'grace' in a religious context. Other more familiar words, such as 'forgiveness' or 'mercy', may be understood very differently from how they are by those steeped in their faith communities. Trained directors will have learned to have their spiritual antennae well tuned to notice when someone is describing something that has theological connotations. A person may describe the daily routine of caring for an invalid neighbour with no obligation to do so but simply because 'It's the right thing to do'. Another may recount the generosity of an anonymous work colleague when there was great need. What is going on here? How could this be the Holy Spirit at work in someone's life?

One of the easiest ways to abuse Scripture is to argue from 'proof texts'. Entire world views have been constructed from a single Bible verse. Arguments have been conducted with each side firing proof texts at one another to say opposite things or hold opposing positions. Devotionally, people have built their faith on a few key texts that appeal to them and ignored all the rest. How does the spiritual director avoid reinforcing this attitude to the Bible when we frequently select Scriptures to suit the situation before us? Using Scripture selectively like this is part of the art of spiritual direction. We listen to people's stories and then send them away with a verse on which to meditate, or we ask them to pray with a single verse for a specific length of time. One person recounted to me how he had gone on a Christian holiday where an entire week's talks had been based on a single verse. This had been an altogether positive experience because the speaker opened up the whole of the biblical landscape through that one verse. It is a reminder of the endless depths of treasure contained within God's word. Nevertheless, we need to be careful not to privilege one verse over another, one passage of Scripture over another passage, Gospels over epistles or vice versa – and so on. There should not be privileged parts of Scripture, and in one sense every verse, every sentence is key to the whole. But it is the case that we will always find more meat in, say, John 3.16 than in the whole of the early chapters of 1 Chronicles, though there is food for thought here too if we are prepared to look. But as the writer Northrop Frye pointed out, 'the immediate context of the sentence is as likely to be three hundred pages off as to be the next or preceding sentence.' Each sentence can lead us into the whole like a candle into a vast labyrinth.[3] We are not aiming to build up a cosy collection of favourite texts but to enable Christian disciples to inhabit the Scriptures in a fulsome way.

If we are going to take the whole of Scripture seriously we have to acknowledge that there are difficult parts as well – parts that will make us feel uncomfortable and parts that cut us to the quick as they address us directly where it matters. Sometimes it will be a shrewd director who points us to the hard passages; sometimes we will just find ourselves there. After all, if we are getting to know Jesus and therefore meditating on the things he said, we will find that he said some hard things too. Always, however, if we are open to hearing, the Holy Spirit will speak to us through the difficult, strange and uncongenial passages as well as the rest. When John ate the scroll in Revelation he found that despite being sweet initially, it was bitter in his stomach (Rev. 10.10).

Flawed images

Our images of God have to be constantly shattered and rebuilt. Time after time we have to relearn what God is like, only to find later that this image also has become fossilized into an idol and has to go. We are especially prone to fall back on the idea that somehow we have to earn God's approval. We think God is disapproving, out to get us even and liable to be critical rather than delighted to have our company.[4] Yet God in the Scriptures is consistently merciful, gracious, faithful, forgiving and steadfast in love. We may read this over and over again and never really believe it until we have experienced it to be true in our own lives. One of the most important tasks of spiritual direction is to come to the place of knowing, in our own experience, that God is these things. Only then will we truly desire to hear him speaking to us as a God who is for us and not against us. It is as we learn to put aside our fears, our judgementalism of others and of ourselves, our blaming, our egocentricity and our persistence in trying to earn God's approval that we are set free to hear the Spirit's voice speaking to us. Only then will the word of God be good news for us.[5] The Scriptures give us permission to take conscious ownership of our personal story at every level and show us that God will use all of it, even the negative parts of our story to weave healing into us and give us life.

To pick up where this chapter began, we will discover that this was also true of the men and women who appear in the Scriptures. Each one of them is flawed in some way and yet God loves them and uses

49

them. They in turn know God and in various ways discern the divine purposes, though sometimes it takes a long time and many attempts. Do you have a Bible hero? Read the story again and discover who that hero really was. Take David, for example: the idealized king of Israel, a mighty warrior and, as the Bible itself says, 'a man after God's own heart' (1 Sam. 13.14). Yet David was an adulterer and a murderer, showed favouritism within his family and disobeyed God's specific commands. Or Abraham, who 'set out, not knowing where he was going' because he lived by faith (Heb. 11.8). He lied and dragged his wife Sarah into a humiliating situation not once but twice (Gen 12.20). Joseph, who became second in command in the mighty nation of Egypt and saved his people from disaster, grew through many trials and tribulations into the wise and discerning leader who met his treacherous brothers with compassion. But he didn't start out that way. He was arrogant and insensitive, and his brothers and even his father bridled at his foolishness. Although today the apostles are held up as the foundational figures of the early Church and have been portrayed in literature and tradition as wonderful saints, the Gospels tell another story, reminding us that they doubted, misunderstood, fell out among themselves and in every single case ran away in Jesus' hour of need. Even the apostle Paul, author of so much of the New Testament, quarrelled with his co-workers and by his own admission struggled with a 'thorn . . . in the flesh' (2 Cor. 12.7). To ignore these aspects of biblical characters is to close down the Scriptures as helping us come to terms with ourselves. We need to let go of the desire to turn the men and women of the Bible into untouchable heroes and heroines if they are to help us with our own discipleship. As Frederick Buechner has commented:

> They speak, this huge gathering of people who crowd the pages of the Bible. They listen. They emerge if we in turn listen to them, not as allegorical embodiments of Goodness and Badness but as flesh-and-blood men and women who no less ambiguously than the rest of us are good one day, bad the next, and occasionally both at once.[6]

But if we come to them seeking to discern how God can work in human lives to bring life and hope, we have more than enough to work with.

5

Stories

———•◆•———

Everyone, from the oldest to the youngest, loves stories. We make them up, tell them, read them, listen to them, identify with them (or not), and some of us write them or act them out. Even if it is only describing what we did yesterday, all of us are capable of relating a story. Spiritual direction is as much about telling our stories through a God-shaped lens as anything else we might think of when describing it.

Scripture plays a key part in providing us with this God-shaped lens. N. T. Wright has described the Bible as a drama in five acts. It has an overarching story covering the working out of God's plan for God's world. We are living in the last act in Wright's framework and we each have a role in this great drama.[1] The role involves the story of our lives. Each day adds to the story and invites us to live more reflectively so that we grow in awareness of God within our story and ourselves within God's story. Most of us reflect by talking about our day formally or informally but we can take this a step further, for 'theology by heart' is a recognized way of doing theological reflection wherein spiritual direction may find a natural home. Letters, journalling, spiritual autobiography and other texts contribute to the weaving of our stories in God's own. Such written documents are dialogical in that they represent conversations with other perspectives as well as their own. A common spiritual practice that many directors encourage is journalling, which adds another stage of reflection to the events that fill our days. Elaine Graham, Heather Walton and Frances Ward trace 'theology by heart' back to the Psalms, where poetry and prayer addressed to God, as for example in Psalm 139, turn to the inward life.[2]

Most of us simply tell our stories verbally to our spiritual directors and both of us then reflect on God's part in the narrative. Telling a story creates space: 'We can dwell in a story, walk around, find our own place. The story confronts but does not oppress; the story inspires but does not manipulate. The story invites us to an encounter, a dialog, a mutual sharing.'[3] The most freeing aspect of working with the stories of the Bible as we reflect on our own stories is the discovery that we find our story to be held within God's story. We are released from looking for where God fits in to our lives and to discovering that we have a place in God's great overarching story. Far from restricting us to getting our story 'right', this truth will expand our vision and deepen our experience of the Lord in the everyday. To acknowledge that our personal story is contained in God's story is not about honouring the specifically religious parts of our story alone. All of our lives are held in God's hands and each moment is graced with God's loving presence, whether or not we are conscious of God. Eastern Orthodox Christians believe that worship is going on in heaven all the time, and when they gather to worship they are simply joining in the flow. Since God uses language to communicate with us, we should be growing in awareness of how everyday conversation can reveal something of God to us. Jesus often used parables. They are in the main not about religious concepts but everyday things told in homely language – 'he told them many things in parables' (Matt. 13.3). As we hear or read these stories again we are listening to God telling us stories and we find that we are in them!

In spiritual direction we are engaged in telling our stories, and as directors we are listening to them and seeking to discern with the narrator where God is present.

Silence through pauses and what is not said is an essential component of storytelling – the spaces in between, the gaps, the punctuation. In God's spacious world there is room to pause, to breathe, to ponder. So many of us live our lives with no punctuation and wonder why we are constantly out of breath. The stories in the Bible are often characterized by a certain reticence. They have a spare, even austere quality to them. There is much that is not said. The blanks invite us in. We can walk around and discover where we fit in. St Ignatius made excellent use of this quality in the way he used the Scriptures with his disciples. He invited them to imagine the scenery, to use their senses to enter into the scene – what could they see, smell, hear and so on. At the end of a prayer time using the imagination, he invited the disciples to have a conversation with Jesus about what had gone on during the prayer.

Imagination

The Scriptures are full of imagination. Image after image tells us what God is like: a mighty wind, a roaring ocean, an eagle fluttering over its young, a pillar of flame, a shepherd, a door, a woman searching for lost coins. Similes and metaphors tumble over themselves to enlighten the imaginations of our hearts to open us to God. The Psalms paint pictures with words. Jesus told parables that invite us to enter their world while his sayings are full of memorable images. Paul in his letters struggles to find words and uses images like the body, an athlete, farmers and seed. Many of these everyday images are embedded in stories. God gave us stories to enlarge our hearts and increase our capacity to know the living Word.

Walter Brueggemann defines imagination as 'the capacity to entertain, host, trust and respond to images of reality (God and the world) that are out beyond conventional dominant reason'.[4] As Christians we have committed ourselves to something we cannot yet see. 'Blessed are those who have not seen and yet have come to believe', said Jesus to doubting Thomas (John 20.29); 'we hope for what we do not see', wrote St Paul (Rom. 8.25).

In this context imagination is indispensable. We have to make the connection between what we see and what we do not see, between heaven and earth, between the now and the not yet. Some Christians are deeply suspicious of the imagination, however, and avoid it at all costs. They regard it as untrustworthy, likely to lead us into darkness and ignorance and best left in the nursery until such time as the infant can rely on reason alone. How sad that we who are made in the 'image' of God value our imaginations so little. The research of David Hay and Rebecca Nye concludes that by about the age of nine, most children have learned that spirituality belongs in the realm of fantasy along with the imagination.[5] When I see the rain falling through my kitchen window I see the plants in the garden reaching up thirstily to drink, I see the pond nearby swelling with fresh supplies of water, I see the grass growing lush and green and I am carried in my imagination to see the desert blossoming like a rose. Everything I describe is in my imagination, but is it any less true for originating there? I can point to various authorities that will test what I see and help me filter out truth from untruth. In the same way the Scriptures ground our imaginations as well as our minds and hearts where truth lies, and if we entrust ourselves to them, why should our imaginations not be fruitful?

Stories can help us to wonder. Godly play has made a huge contribution here with its wondering approach to retelling some of the biblical stories to children.[6] It is perhaps not surprising that adults have found Godly play captivating too. Often adulthood brings in its wake a loss of wonder. By the time children enter their teens they will have learned that it is not cool to be amazed at anything, no matter how stupendous it might be. The fact that there are millions of galaxies – so what? That you are unique and so am I? No comment! Wonder is something we have to relearn along with spontaneity and intuition. A story invites us to stop, look and listen and enjoy. We may imagine the crowds hanging on to Jesus' every word as he told them stories, so that when the punchline came they were stunned and speechless. No doubt that is what Jesus intended because those moments when we are caught unawares offer the possibility of redefining reality and seeing something new. Wonder is a gift worth cherishing. It is just a hair's breadth away from praise, and praise opens the door of heaven.

Often we find ourselves revisiting parts of our childhood in spiritual direction in order to rediscover wonder. We will find that it is not just of benefit to ourselves but that it is liberating for others too. Is it not easier to wonder at a sunset when someone else is standing beside us? Helping others to see, to wonder and to move to praise is a gift in itself. Think of how the shepherds who knelt in wonder at the manger have inspired countless congregations gathered for a Christmas service to find their voice to praise God.

Metaphor

The use of stories invites us to consider the place of metaphor as a means of understanding what God is like. The Bible is full of such metaphors for they help us glimpse what cannot be fully explained by human language. We use similes and metaphors all the time in everyday speech: 'She has a heart of gold', 'It was raining cats and dogs', 'They ran like the wind'. A foreign visitor unfamiliar with the

English language might wonder about cats and dogs falling from the sky for they are unfamiliar with the metaphorical mode of expression commonly understood by the English in this context. This point is all the more relevant when we come to the Bible, which is no longer known and understood in public parlance. People do not know the stories of the Old and New Testaments in the way that once enabled biblical phrases and images to be used in everyday speech without a second thought. It is one reason why it is more difficult to sing some of the older hymns in church today – they are full of images and metaphors that have their origins in little-read parts of the Bible and therefore do not carry meaning for those singing.

The use of simile and metaphor is a well-known method of helping someone understand what would otherwise remain opaque and beyond reach. Where theological concepts are concerned it is particularly necessary, and theologians have always employed metaphor to speak of God. To begin to read the Bible is to enter a world interconnected by the language of simile and metaphor. From the very beginning, when God planted a garden and walked there in the cool of the day, we are dealing in metaphorical language. One image builds on another; so much depends on a background of understood imagery. When the first letter of Peter refers to believers as 'a chosen race, a royal priesthood, a holy nation, God's own people', his audience would have had a rich background of Old Testament imagery to interpret his meaning. Many of the New Testament letters are written to explain concepts embedded in Jewish thinking that required re-imaging in the light of Christ's coming, and so new images build on old and we can almost feel the writers struggling at times to find words that will express the inexpressible.

This applies to both the Old and New Testaments. Reading about the words and actions of Jesus without the Old Testament is to strip them of their context. It is not just his parables that are inviting us to see what God is like through metaphorical stories, nor his sayings that begin 'The kingdom of God is like . . .' (Matt. 13; Luke 13). We have not only to enter Jesus' everyday world that was saturated in the imagery of the Old Testament but also grasp the newness of what he revealed about God. In one sense Jesus himself, as the Word made flesh, is the living metaphor who demonstrates in his life, death and resurrection what God is truly like.

When John Bunyan wrote his great allegory *The Pilgrim's Progress* in the seventeenth century, he could assume a much greater fluency of biblical language in everyone who might pick up his book to read it. He had to defend his use of metaphor, however, against some of his contemporaries who disapproved of using metaphor to speak of God. He did so in his verse preface on the grounds that this is in fact how God speaks to us:

> But must I want solidness, because
> By metaphors I speak? Were not God's laws,
> His Gospel laws, in olden times held forth
> By shadows, types and metaphors? Yet loath
> Will any sober man be to find fault
> With them, lest he be found for to assault
> The Highest Wisdom. No; he rather stoops
> And seeks to find out what by pins and loops,
> By calves and sheep, by heifers and by rams,
> By birds and herbs, and by the blood of lambs,
> God speaketh to him; and happy is he
> That finds the light and grace that in them be.[7]

Bunyan was an uneducated tinker. How could he have acquired eyes to see and an imagination to dream like this? He had learned to inhabit the Scriptures so that he saw signs of God everywhere and was able to make connections between life and the word of God. When we learn to listen for God's word in the Scriptures we too will learn how to listen for God's word in every conversation, every blade of grass on which we tread and every face we encounter. We discover that truth and meaning are to be found in God's story and we learn to see their signs. Learning to read the signs means developing a prophetic vision and some of us will, perhaps, find our voice and speak out on behalf of the voiceless. We will learn above all to find our place in God's story.

We may have to work that bit harder to understand the significance of 'birds and herbs' and the 'blood of lambs' but it is vital that we do in order to be able to enter the world of the Bible for ourselves and to be free to move around in its atmosphere. It is a task worth persevering with and one in which a spiritual director may prove an invaluable guide and companion.

Telling our stories

When all is said and done, spiritual direction involves telling our stories. It must be our own story for we cannot tell anyone else's for them. At the end of John's Gospel Jesus indicates to Peter what will happen to him, and Peter asks Jesus about the fate of the beloved disciple. Jesus refuses to divulge information to Peter about someone else and gently rebukes him: 'what is that to you?' (John 21.22). C. S. Lewis makes the point beautifully in more than one of the Narnia stories when one of the children asks Aslan about someone else. In *The Horse and His Boy*, for example, Shasta asks if it was the lion himself who had wounded Aravis. 'Child,' replied Aslan, 'I am telling you your own story, not hers. I tell no one any story but his own.'[8] Rowan Williams discusses this theme in *The Lion's World*: God addresses me and not someone else.[9] The spiritual director's job is to get out of the way so that we may hear the living Word and respond.

It is interesting to discuss novels and TV dramas with friends who have certain ideas about the way stories should end. I love the mystery of ambiguity in a story. Did he do it or didn't he? Did they get back together after their reconciliation or go their separate ways? The story of Jonah in the Bible has no satisfactory ending. Jonah has fallen out with God as he sat under the unpredictable plant and God reprimanded him, ending with a question: 'And should I not be concerned about Nineveh, that great city, in which there are more than a hundred and twenty thousand people who do not know their right hand from their left, and also many animals?' (Jonah 4.11). We are not given Jonah's response to that question but are left to imagine it for ourselves. The storyteller has withheld it so that we have space to provide our own. There is an element of unknowing in spiritual direction that prevents the director becoming a fixer and the directee becoming dependent on someone else's insights. Far from filling someone in with our knowledge about the Bible, Christian teaching on this or that, we are reminded that we do not know what God may be doing in the life of another, and that it is between that person and God alone. Indeed we may well be regarded as an icon of the mystery of God's dealings with us – a mystery that is for us only.

There is another unsatisfactory ending in Scripture that may be far more alarming than the minor prophet Jonah. Mark's Gospel ends abruptly with the women fleeing the empty tomb in terror. What is going on here? Didn't Mark write to convince people that Jesus was the Messiah? Why is there no triumphant resurrection appearance that silences all doubt and questioning? So uncomfortable is the ending that soon other writers began to supply endings of their own. Many Bibles contain two of these, a long one and a short one. But perhaps Mark intended his Gospel to finish mid-sentence. Perhaps he meant others to supply their own endings, though maybe he hoped they would be endings wrestled out in prayer and that their authors would keep them to themselves and God. It is as if Mark is reaching out from his page to say: 'Take the pen and write the conclusion to this earth-shattering truth yourself. God has broken into this world; will you allow the Lord to break into yours?'

So much spiritual direction is about the divine invitation to us to respond to God in our lives. What will that response look like? Only you, only I can say. It will be our own personal response and may be too deep for words in any case.

Knowing the stories too well

'I write to you, not because you do not know the truth, but because you know it' (1 John 2.21). There is a different problem that is the opposite of not knowing the Bible terrain, and that is overfamiliarity with it. A person who has been a Christian for many years and read and reread the Bible may struggle to find new insight in its pages. Where is the freshness of encounter when a person has heard the narrative so many times already? Part of the answer lies in the nature of the biblical narrative, for one of the functions of stories is to invite us to consider familiar things in a new light. Recall the parables of Jesus and the way they utilize ordinary things like bread and fields and seeds – things that are with us every day but that we had failed to notice. We are invited to look again and discover that far from being matters of indifference to us, they have something profound to teach us; far from being ordinary, they are of critical importance. Such ordinary things have the capacity to teach us to pray. In his book on prayer, Richard Foster writes about using the ordinary in prayer. We can pray while doing ordinary things like driving to work or standing in a queue. We can also look at ordinary things as signposts to God that lead us into prayer in daily life. A loaf of bread, running water, a moving crowd of people and so many other ordinary things prompt us to speak to God in our hearts about them and about the concerns of which they remind us.[10]

Over and over Christians who have lived with the Scriptures for years claim to see new things, new truths and new challenges in the Bible as they read. Passages they have read many times jump out at them. It is as though they have never noticed this or that verse before. Our lives grow and develop. Circumstances change and we need new resources to meet them. This is when the Scriptures help us to discover fresh springs of water ever gushing up in newness. The well is indeed very deep (John 4.11).

We may need help to return to familiar parts of Scripture that have become dry from repeated use. If this seems a contradiction it is worth considering the role of repetition in prayer and Bible reading. Repetition need not be the sterile, boring practice associated with rote learning and mindless repeating of words. It took me a long time to discover there was a world of difference between chanting my six-times table and repeating the Psalms aloud on a daily basis. All the same, both aid memory and lead to insight and good practice. Teachers and prayer guides have recognized the value of returning to well-trodden territory in prayer and meditation to deepen rather than deaden insight and understanding (see Chapter 7). Scholars of literary criticism talk of reading with a second naiveté. We need to find ways to recapture the wonder and impact of reading something for the first time.

Repetition has other uses as well. Small children will listen to the same story or watch the same film over and over, never tiring of the same lines, the same images before them. Students of child development maintain that this is a vital aspect of their growth and development. Through the repetition they learn to construct reality and to build language. Interestingly, I noticed how certain phrases from books and films became household catchphrases while our young son was growing and they remain so today. 'Don't forget the crackers, Gromit' has multiple connotations in our home to this day!

There are many ways to make our way back to reading Scripture with the thrill of that first time around. Trying a different translation, a dramatic reading or even learning the words and reciting them out loud all have the potential to arrest that sense of overfamiliarity. One friend listens to a recording and moves her body to express the words spoken. Another draws them or paints while meditating. Many have been helped by artistic depictions of biblical stories, one of the most well-known being Henri Nouwen's book-length meditation on Rembrandt's painting *The Return of the Prodigal Son*.[11]

Seeing things

The Scriptures invite us to see the world in a new way and to see our place in it in new ways. How do we recover this sense of expectation that God will surprise us, shock us into seeing things the way the godhead sees them and call us into ever new adventures? We are apt to hear another's story and wish it were our own. It seems so much grander, more exciting, more action-packed than our small world. We do not have to be influential, important or well travelled, however, to know fullness of life in God's kingdom. One of my favourite characters of faith was St Bede, who was a biblical scholar, linguist, astronomer, mathematician and poet. He wrote the first history of the Christian Church in the British Isles yet he hardly ever left the monastery where he had spent most of his life from the age of seven. The world came to him and he drank it in, pondered it and found in it the glory of God. Another wise character, the American writer Henry David Thoreau, wrote of having 'travelled a good deal in Concord' (a small village in New England where he spent his life).[12] If we are prepared to travel widely in the Scriptures as explorers, we too will find enough to fill us with wonder and awe to last a lifetime. The writer and mystic Annie Dillard can write page after page of gripping prose about a single tiny insect that opens our eyes to the depths of creation. How? She has learned to look and see what is under her feet and all around her and know that it has something to say to her.[13]

6

Themes in Scripture and spiritual direction

In her book *Spiritual Direction*, Janet Ruffing quotes one spiritual director who described direction as being 'like panning for gold'. He went on:

> A directee comes and together we dip into the stream of their life and pull up all kinds of things. Rocks of all sizes ... all kinds of conflicts and problems, then all of a sudden some fleck or nugget of pure gold emerges into view at the bottom of the pan as we swirl the water around, emptying out the rocks.[1]

These flecks and nuggets of gold are the experience of grace and the Holy Spirit in a person's life and they are deeply valuable and significant. One of the tasks of directors is to help directees connect these flecks and nuggets to the Christian tradition and make sense of them in the light of faith. Skilled directors will enable directees to see how their stories fit into God's story. Along the way themes from the tradition will emerge in the stories – themes that Scripture has the capacity to illuminate and enlarge. In this chapter there is only space to flag up some of the universal themes that all who desire to know God and themselves better will encounter at some point in their praying.

Questions

I remember describing an experience to my spiritual director in what I thought were – commendably – measured tones only to receive her response: 'What makes you angry?' It took many years to answer that question, and it sent me back to the Gospels to study the things that made Jesus angry and the way he responded.

Asking questions is fundamental to human nature. It is how we have made advances in knowledge and skills; it has led to exploration of the human mind and found expression in physical adventure. Questions have led to artistic expression of human searchings and lie at the heart of many a conversation. The young toddler who has just discovered speech asks 'Why?' and the old woman dying looks back and questions what she has experienced and observed in her long life. We navigate our lives with questions both profound and mundane. The Bible is often assumed to be a book of answers but it is full of people who ask questions of life just as we do because it is a book about us as well as God. These men and women are not afraid to ask God some hard questions: 'How long, O LORD?' (Ps. 13.1); 'Why, O LORD?' (Ps. 10.1); 'Why have you forsaken me?' (Ps. 22.1); 'Who then is this, that even the wind and the sea obey him?' (Mark 4.41); 'What are human beings that you are mindful of them, mortals that you care for them?' (Ps. 8.4). The Psalms especially demonstrate the human impulse to question where matters of justice are concerned and plead their cause with a God who seems not to be playing fair. All this is the stuff of spiritual direction and offers rich resources for anyone wrestling with questions. Rarely is there a straight answer, for it is by sitting with the questions and waiting on God's action in our lives that we grow in faith and trust.

We may not have considered the fact that God asks questions of us also in our walk of faith. There are some penetrating questions that come to us from God in the Scriptures. At the very outset of the human story God asks Adam, as the first humans hide in shame, 'Where are you?' (Gen. 3.9). 'What are you doing here, Elijah?' (1 Kings 19.9) is a question that puts us on the spot and shakes us out of our complacency. Elijah had recently triumphed over the prophets of Baal only to crumble at the threat of Queen Jezebel and flee for his life into the desert.

Jesus had the habit of responding to questions put to him with another question, and his answers continue to challenge us to respond: 'What do you want me to do for you?' (Mark 10.51); 'Do you want to be made well?' (John 5.6); 'Do you also wish to go away?' (John 6.67). Often he refused to answer his critics who questioned him and instead asked: 'What is written in the law? What do you read there?' (Mark 10.26). Good spiritual directors will emulate Jesus' questioning style and ask directees questions rather than try to provide the answers. 'Where has God been in your life since we last met?' may be the only words required for the Holy Spirit to get to work.

Desert

Sooner or later the majority of people who try to pray will experience the desert. One person has described it as if he was writing a postcard to God that said simply: 'Wish you were here.'

The desert is a provocative image, having both literal and figurative meaning for many people. Some go in search of literal deserted places to be alone with God in prayer, emulating Jesus' own practice of going away to a lonely place.[2]

For others it has a powerful symbolic meaning. We may live in a remote place and feel that lack of resources make life a desert. We may have a strong sense of God's absence and feel that we are in a desert place. We may go to church and feel no connection with what happens there and feel the lack of Christian community as being in a desert. The image of the desert is a vivid description of what happens when prayer dries up and seems to go no further than the ceiling.

Both the Christian and Jewish faiths were born out of the desert – key events such as the Exodus and the giving of the law take place in the wilderness. These events also shaped the mission of Jesus and hence the New Testament. Every significant leader was shaped in the desert: Abraham, Moses, the whole people of Israel, Jacob, Elijah, the prophets, John the Baptist, the apostle Paul and above all Jesus and the early Church. It is not surprising, then, that desert imagery figures large in the biblical material. Indeed in a real sense the God of the Bible is the God of the desert.[3]

Since the desert is more of an experience than a place for most people, it is felt as disorientating, and this makes us vulnerable, especially as it usually comes unbidden and unwanted. This is where Scripture has so many riches to help us. It is first the very language of prayer in the Bible: 'My soul thirsts for you . . . as in a dry and weary land where there is no water' (Ps. 63.1).

The language of the cross and of suffering is desert language: 'My God, my God why have you forsaken me?' (Ps. 22.1; Matt. 27.46; Mark 15.34). And perhaps more than anything it is the place of waiting: 'I wait for the LORD, my soul waits, and in his word I hope' (Ps. 130.5) or 'It is good that one should wait quietly for the salvation of the LORD' (Lam. 3.26). We hate waiting and we cannot find anything more countercultural than such exhortations, but this is the culture of Scripture, designed to help us live well wherever we find ourselves.

In our fast-moving success-orientated culture many people live with constant insecurity and a sense of powerlessness. It is in the desert that we learn a different kind of security that weans us off our false props – our addictions and dependencies – and where, if we dare to trust and let go, we will find true freedom. Further themes to explore are power and what this looks like from God's perspective; freedom and what it really means; and judgement too, for in our recognition of our emptiness God meets us with mercy. The primary call of the desert is to be alone with God and to seek God absolutely, and it means the abandonment of everything except the desire for God. As a result our priorities will look very different seen from the perspective of the desert.

Scripture shows us that Jesus made the desert a place of prayer. He used Scripture there to combat Satan and to find nourishment and strength as well as wisdom and insight. The Desert Fathers and Mothers saw themselves as recapitulating the experience of Jesus in the desert as he battled with temptation, and they often referred to '40 days' as a description of their own endurance. In the British Isles, the early Celtic Christians, who knew about and admired the desert dwellers, treated the remote and barren islands off the coast of the mainland as their desert places, where they too spent long hours in prayer and fought with evil spirits.

Whatever our desert place is, be it lonely, rough, fearful or all of these, we may know that Jesus has been there already and hallowed it.

Silence

We have all encountered words that feel as though they have been uttered too quickly without much thought or formation on the part of the speaker. They sound glib and even hollow, though in themselves they may be true. Jesus warned his hearers to be careful about the words they spoke 'for by your words you will be justified, and by your words you will be condemned' (Matt. 12.36–37). These are words for every spiritual director to hear and tremble at. Jesus himself, however, shows us how to avoid offering mere platitudes to those who seek us out for direction.

> In the morning, while it was still very dark, he got up and went out to a deserted place, and there he prayed. And Simon and his companions hunted for him. When they found him, they said to him, 'Everyone is searching for you!' He answered, 'Let us go on to the neighbouring towns, so that I may proclaim the message there also; for that is what I came out to do.' (Mark 1.35–38)

Prayer in solitude was essential to Jesus' being able to speak God's word to the people. First of all he needed to hear God speaking to him in the silence so that he could discern what God would have him say. As a result he knew where to go and what to say as he continued to live in God's presence moment by moment. This was the pattern of his life. In the silence we too may learn to listen so that we may speak a word of wisdom or truth to another at the right moment. Powerful words may emerge from the silence to sow seeds that will bring forth fruit in their time. Such are life-giving words that bring healing and hope where they are needed.

There is an important place for words that have come into existence out of the silence, and this too is a biblical theme. On Mount Horeb Elijah hid in his cave while outside there was an earthquake followed by a mighty wind and then a fire (1 Kings 19). But God was not in any of these. Afterwards came 'a sound of sheer silence' (v. 12) or 'a still small voice' (v. 12 KJV). Now at last Elijah came to hear the word of the Lord to him, with its challenge and renewal of his prophetic calling.

For the desert Fathers and Mothers silence was of the essence of their existence. It was 'the soil in which words of life were cultivated',[4] and while we may not be called to emulate their lifestyle, their experience of God in the silence and solitude of the desert continues to challenge us in our busy, noisy world. This is not a personality issue, though it is true that extraverts will find silence and solitude more of a challenge than introverts, to whom both come naturally. The verse in Ecclesiastes that reminds us there is 'a time to keep silence, and a time to speak' is for all of us, whatever our personality type (Eccles. 3.7).

Guidance and the will of God

Christians often tie themselves in knots over questions of guidance, and the word of God suffers much abuse in the process. It is not a lucky dip, a kind of Christian horoscope that will tell us exactly what to do in any given situation. That there are clear commands is not in dispute, but in God's desire that we grow into maturity as human beings he has given us many choices and opportunities to work out for ourselves what is best for us. Spiritual direction is bound to throw up questions of what God would have us do in a given situation. Certainly the struggle to understand what God is saying at times of suffering and crisis is part of the mystery of faith that seems to ask much of us. Sometimes simply talking aloud with a listening companion is enough to clarify our muddled thoughts, but meditating on the Scriptures is a tried and tested way to lead us in the best direction. A spiritual director will be able to suggest passages to help so that we are not left to open the Bible at random and hope it speaks to us. Helpful passages are not necessarily those that mirror our own experience. It may be some of the big themes, like the Exodus, the Covenant or the entry into the Promised Land, that open our spiritual eyes. It is also important to notice how God guides others in Scripture. While there is dramatic divine intervention on occasion, it is also the case that God guides through ordinary means, such as the wisdom of an older person or discussion between two people. Guidance in Scripture is a process and can take time. It took the Israelites 40 years in the desert to learn God's ways, despite a dramatic deliverance from Egypt at the outset. Natural and supernatural guidance come together in the Incarnation for although the Word became flesh through a special act of God, Jesus was born to a human mother in the ordinary way. He grew up in the way that all humans grow and while he had miraculous powers of healing and control over nature, he did not simply pole-vault every obstacle in his way. He himself wrestled with God on the night he was betrayed. God works the divine purposes out with us through the warp and weft of our ordinary lives. When we lament the fact that God has not directly intervened it is not because we are not loved but because we are loved so much that we were created to be mature human beings who reflect the divine image in our persons, rather than automatons programmed to obey. Reflecting on his father's suicide and the way God directs our lives, Frederick Buechner commented:

> God acts in history and in your and my brief histories not as the puppeteer who sets the scene and works the strings but rather as the great director who no matter what role fate casts us in conveys to us somehow from the wings, if we have our eyes, ears and hearts open and sometimes even if we don't, how we can play those roles in a way to enrich and ennoble and hallow the whole vast drama of things including our own small but crucial parts in it.[5]

Risk

As the above paragraphs indicate, all this is very risky. A key element of spiritual direction is risk. The God we encounter in the Scriptures and in Jesus Christ is not a tame God ready to do our bidding and conforming to our ideas of what God should be. If we are seeking the reality of the living God we must be prepared to be stirred, challenged, shaken to the very foundations of our being and willing to change in order to grow. This is true both of director and directee. We take a risk every time we reveal something of ourselves to another. Articulating the depths of our hearts and minds to a director involves risk but so does speaking into the life of another person. The director takes a risk here too. The process is risky because entering into spiritual direction is never meant to be a retreat from reality into some kind of safe haven. It may be about the journey inwards but this is never the final resting place. Ultimately spiritual direction is about sending people back into the world they have come from, in order to find God there and often with a challenge to act, speak out or change their behaviour. God and God's activity in human lives is not confined to an hour of spiritual direction any more than the Holy Spirit is limited to church gatherings to reveal the divine presence. Risk is built into the Christian life but we are never abandoned to our own devices. There is plenty of material in the Scriptures to help us navigate the risky waters, for here we see the Lord calling people to follow in ways that put everything on the line for God's sake.

When people met Jesus and responded to his word it often meant a complete change to their future lives. The man born blind, for example, could no longer rely on others to lead him (John 9); Zacchaeus could no longer cheat his way through life (Luke 19.1–10).

The disciples left everything behind when they heard Jesus calling them to follow him, and we see them stumbling and falling but risking everything because they had been gripped by him. Simon Peter summed up their attitude: 'Lord, to whom can we go? You have the words of eternal life' (John 6.68). Not everyone was willing to take the risk. The rich ruler, for example, turned away sorrowful (Mark 10.17–22). Others, like Nicodemus, were cautious, but gradually grew in confidence (cf. John 3.2; 7.50; 19.39). When the Gerasene demoniac was healed he wanted to go with Jesus, but he was sent home instead to witness to what Jesus had done for him (Mark 5.1–20). In Mark 1.21–28 the evil spirits resisted Jesus. This passage shows us that it is important to listen not only for what is lovely and gracious but also for what is challenging. We will need to pray for the self-knowledge it may be inviting us to explore, and yield to Christ, trusting that he always wants good things for us.

Jesus does not step into our lives against our will but if we ask him he can turn the hardness of our hearts, our deafness, our coldness, our resistance, to an attitude of loving attentiveness and receptiveness to his word. Resistance plays a key role in spiritual direction because when we begin to open up to the work of the Holy Spirit within us, what Scripture calls the 'self' (Rom. 6.6; Eph. 4.22; Col. 3.9) digs in his heels and resists change.

Fear

Closely related to risk is fear for this lies at the root of our unwillingness to change. Every human being feels fear to a greater or lesser degree. The first humans hid from God because they were afraid (Gen. 3.10), and we have continued to run from the Lord ever since, refusing to believe in the unconditional love offered to us. Indeed fear is so deeply embedded in our human nature that it is not surprising that the most frequent command in Scripture is 'Do not be afraid'. The words thread their way through Old and New Testaments, uttered by prophets, angels, apostles and directly by God. Jesus frequently told his disciples not to be afraid, or asked them why they were (Mark 4.40). Here was the Lord of glory, present with them and demonstrating his sovereignty over Creation, and they were filled with fear! How many people have held back from saying 'yes' to God because of fear? Fear constricts, blinds and holds us in chains. It causes us to refuse the call to live life to the full and prevents us speaking out on behalf of what is just and true. Scripture is full of promises that God is with us but more than this it narrates the experience of men and women who dared believe it. It also reveals the true character of God, contrary to the false ideas and images many people hold in their minds. In Matthew's account of the Transfiguration it is significant that Jesus tells his disciples not to be afraid, and God says 'Listen to him'. As we listen for the life-giving word of God we find healing balm for all our fears. Here God was telling the disciples that 'This is my Son, the Beloved, with whom I am well pleased' (Matt. 3.17 and parallels). 'Who is God for me?' is a classic question asked in spiritual direction that if answered honestly and in conversation with the Scriptures can begin to unlock some of the depths of God's love and care for us as creatures. In this way a healthy awe may dispel our false images of God and with them our fears. Fear more than anything else requires someone else to walk with us with encouragement and a trustworthy presence as we face the things that bind us and keep us from breaking free. With the proviso that some of our fears are rooted in terrible experiences and need more than a friendly companion, where spiritual direction is concerned there may be great opportunities to overcome our fearful attitudes and grow in faith.

7

Models of relating in spiritual direction

During the mid-twentieth century some Christians in communist China found themselves imprisoned for their faith. One of them had managed to smuggle in a single page of his Bible. It was passed round from one prisoner to another so that each one could feed on it as food for a starving soul. If you were among those prisoners, what would you do when it came to your turn? There are many models of spiritual direction in the Church that in turn rely on different ways of feeding on God's word. In this chapter we explore some of the major spiritual traditions of guidance still valuable today.

As I have been writing, the spiritual directors who have accompanied me over the years have often been in my mind. They have all been different and worked from different models of directing. By now most of those reading this book will have forming in their minds an image of what a spiritual director is like, even if they have not experienced spiritual direction. Eugene Peterson described Reuben, his first spiritual director, in one of his books.[1] Reuben assumed a stance of wonderment and in his company Peterson likewise began to enter into wonder. As Reuben listened to him Peterson became aware that he was himself an aspect of the mystery of God that was a mystery not to be fitted into an already prepared programme. He wrote: 'For [Reuben's] attentiveness was not to me, as such, but to God. Slowly his attitude began to infect me – I gradually began to lose interest in myself and got interested in God in me.'[2]

Listening is very important in our culture. It is at the heart of all therapy. It is fundamental to spiritual direction. It is so embedded that we are prone to parody it – 'I hear what you are saying' – and yet continue to listen superficially rather than at depth. It remains the case that many of us do not feel listened to. Spiritual direction may be one of the few hours where we are offered complete and uncon-ditional attention. Being listened to at depth may be the beginning of transformation.

We live in a therapeutic culture where we are prone to construct God as an empathetic version of ourselves – a vulnerable deity who gets alongside us. While not necessarily abandoning these attributes we need to be aware of the extent to which our culture influences our ideas about God. It is therefore important to acknowledge that we come to the Bible with the lenses of our culture and may need to remove our default spectacles to see afresh. With such awareness the Scriptures can help us transcend culturally bound images of God and also our own understanding of ourselves. We find ourselves, our true selves, as we stand before Jesus Christ crucified.

Christians have a further layer of interpretation stemming from the particular tradition they inhabit. Our church background and initial introduction to the Christian faith determines how we approach believing and obeying Christ and also colours our approach to the Scriptures. Whether we wear the spectacles of an Evangelical or Roman Catholic, Pentecostal or Liberal will have an enormous bearing on the place of the Bible in our spiritual life and how we read it. Spiritual directors come from many traditions and their churchmanship is not an issue in directing unless they have been unable to let go of particular shibboleths, in which case they prob-ably ought not to be offering spiritual direction. For people seeking direction, however, it may be a very risky thing to discuss intimate aspects of prayer with someone from a different spiritual tradition. They may worry that their experience may not be valued or their way of relating to God not appreciated. For Evangelicals there may be suspicion of a director who does not have the same high view of Scripture as themselves. They may find that the simple gift of being taken seriously and listened to deeply by a competent director is sufficient to allay fears of being led down a dubious path. There are a number of reasons why people choose directors who are from the same tradition as themselves or, by way of contrast, deliberately look for someone from a different one. They may need the security that the director will be on their 'wavelength', or the director may have been recommended by someone they know and whose judge-ment they trust. On the other hand, any restlessness or dissatisfaction with prayer may propel people to seek out a director who is not from their familiar stable in the hopes that doing so will open up new vistas in prayer and stretch them beyond what feels stale or unsuited to their needs. This may involve new ways of praying with the Bible and fresh interpretations of well-trodden ground. My first spiritual director came from a very different spiritual tradition from my own at that point, and in many ways represented a style of directing that was old fashioned. I persevered because I sensed that this person was someone who prayed and also because I knew I was being listened to. Slowly I began to articulate my longings and struggle where prayer was concerned, and here was someone who both understood and could suggest new ideas that I had never come across before, which stretched me and took me on an adventure in prayer that still goes on.

Names

It is in part a consequence of this possible misunderstanding of the nature of spiritual direction that a number of alternative names for it have arisen in the past 40 years. Each alternative says something about the nature of spiritual direction that provides insight into its character. Some people talk about 'prayer accompaniment', which draws attention to the companionship involved in two people walking the Christian way together. They may refer to spiritual directors as 'spiritual companions' and appreciate the way they work with those seeking to know more of God and his will for them. Nothing here is forced or open to abuse of power and authority. This term also focuses on prayer as being central to spiritual direction.

Others talk of a 'soul friend' and may use the Celtic term *anam chara*. This also denotes a relationship of equals, although in fact the role of the *anam chara* in Celtic Christianity could be one of enormous authority. 'A person without a soul friend is like a body without a head'[3] suggests that such a spiritual director could exercise great authority in others' lives, directing the way they should take as the mind rules the rest of the person. On the other hand, soul friend today is more likely to emphasize the friendship aspect of spiritual direction. It suggests an informal approach where the emphasis is on support and encouragement. The soul friend is one who can help us discern God's voice amid all the other voices clamouring for attention and can help us recognize where God is at work when we do not think we have said anything significant or feel as though nothing is happening. Jesus spoke of the Holy Spirit bringing to remembrance the words he had spoken to his disciples (John 14.26). This happens frequently through the insight of Christian brothers and sisters who have committed to walking the way with us.

'Prayer guide' is commonly found as a way of describing this ministry. Again the prayer aspect is highlighted and the term 'guide' is intended to denote someone who has travelled this way before or who is a little farther on and can point the way to others without forcing them to take a specified route. Just as it is good to have a guide in an unfamiliar place to help us get used to its strange language and sign posts, and to take us round to help us get our bearings, so a prayer guide may walk with us as we learn the grammar of prayer. There is a huge need for people who can show others who are just setting out on their adventure into prayer how to read the maps, which routes are good to take and where there are unseen pitfalls. There is a need for people who have tuned their ears to the whispers of the Holy Spirit in daily life and conversation. 'The wind blows where it chooses and you hear the sound of it, but you do not know where it comes from or where it goes. So it is with everyone who is born of the Spirit' (John 3.8).

'Spiritual mentoring' needs to be mentioned because it may refer to spiritual direction as discussed here or denote a more contem-porary form of mentoring whereby someone who is more experienced at a given skill models, instructs, oversees and trains someone who is still learning and needs greater knowledge and practice to become proficient. It is clearly a model of discipling Christians that is present in the Bible and has been tried and tested in numerous contexts. It is worth noting that mentoring today, like spiritual direction, has taken on a new lease of life in many different contexts.

One term that needs mentioning if only to clear it out of the way is that of 'spiritual counsellor'. Much has been gained from the world of counselling and therapy in terms of process and in the way director and directee relate to each other, but spiritual direction is emphatically not about counselling but about the ongoing journey of faith. Though there may be difficulties along the way, spiritual direction is not usually entered into because of a presenting problem other than struggles in prayer. Too much stress on the counsellor model may make the director look for problems. God is the focus of spiritual direction rather than a problem. Focus on a problem could mean that God is left on the sidelines. A further issue is the nature of the relationship itself, for directors who see themselves as counsellors may overemphasize the importance of remaining detached and so lose the element of soul friendship and companionship that nourishes the director–directee relationship.

Just as the term 'director' has come under the spotlight so has the counterpart 'directee', an unwieldy name for someone wanting to grow in prayer and faith. Some now prefer 'pilgrim' as a more descriptive term and also a more biblical metaphor. It is a reminder that we have to make the spiritual journey ourselves, often putting one foot in front of the other in slow and deliberate fashion as we navigate the path we are on. As with all pilgrimages, we discover companions with whom we can share part of the journey and guides who have trodden the way before us. Whatever terms we choose, the essential fact remains that it is the Holy Spirit who is being sought, and directors must therefore allow 'the Creator to deal directly with the creature and the creature directly with his Creator and Lord', as St Ignatius put it.[4]

Desert Fathers and Mothers

The Desert Fathers and Mothers are especially helpful in helping us understand different meanings of 'word' in spiritual direction. These 'desert dwellers', as they are sometimes called, were men and women who left their settled lives in the cities during the fourth and fifth centuries to seek God in the desert. Although the main thrust for the exodus from the cities was the growing sense that the Church had sold out to the Roman Empire and lost its cutting edge, there were people going into the desert to seek a word from God even before the persecutions had ceased. It was a lay movement and by and large these folk were not learned; but they knew the value of wisdom and so a novice would look for an older monk who could 'give him a word'. Often such older, wiser disciples, known as abbas and ammas, gathered small groups around them in communities and helped the younger monks and nuns to hear God's word to them. They meant three things by 'word', all of which have been discussed earlier. First and foremost they meant the living Word of God, the Lord Jesus Christ. He was the model of salvation whom they sought with all their being. Then they also meant the word in the Scriptures, the written word. Most of them, however, could not read or write and what Scriptures they possessed they learned by heart, for theirs was a largely oral culture. They might have a single Gospel or a fragment of another part of the Bible and, aided by their liturgy, would memorize it and meditate on it over and over until it sank deep into their soul. Third, they meant a spoken word that often flowed out of their meditations on the written word and prayer to the living Word. They were careful with spoken words and might remain silent even when asked for a single one by a pilgrim. There is a story of a respected abba who was visited by the Bishop of Alexandria, who sought a word from the holy man. Instead of coming out of his cell to greet the bishop, the abba remained within. The bishop waited but nothing came. After some days of growing impatience he sent a message. Finally the abba sent a message in return: 'If he is not edified by my silence, he will not be edified by anything I say.' A common expression in the desert was the request: 'Abba, speak a word [*rhema*] to me.' *Rhema* corresponds to the Hebrew *dabar*, which connotes a deed or event announced by a word. Such words as spoken by the Desert Fathers were understood to be inspired by the Holy Spirit and hence carried authority and were only spoken to someone who showed a willingness to put the word into practice. Sometimes it was enough to point to the word of God itself, as St Antony did when some brothers came to him seeking a word to help them discover how to be saved. Antony's response was: 'You have heard Scripture. That should teach you how.'[5] This story is a reminder that the monks of the desert primarily heard rather than read the Scriptures. Every week they met for *synaxis*, the practice of gathering together to hear and recite the Scriptures. They also recited them alone or in small groups in their cells during the week. In addition they meditated on Scripture, mulling it over in their mind, chewing on it and digesting it. The practice of meditation was considered foundational to the monastic life. It was also one of the most effective means of protecting the monk against the snares of evil. Having persuaded a brother to admit to his struggles against temptation, the monk Macarius offered some advice: 'Meditate on the Gospel and the other Scriptures, and if a thought arises within you, never look at it but always look upwards, and the Lord will come at once to your help.' The brother followed his advice and eventually was set free from his temptations. The monks learned that Scripture also helped them overcome their fears and longings and the sheer tedium of much of life in the desert, all familiar experiences of people today despite the very different circumstances. Douglas Burton-Christie makes the point that the principle governing the interpretation of Scripture in the desert was that it was relational. The desert dwellers, in other words, approached the Scriptures with the expectation that it would be transformative.[6]

Silence is a significant feature of desert spirituality. There is a hunger for silence in a perpetually noisy world, yet many remain afraid of it. What part does it play in the Christian life? Ironically it was concern with words that helps to explain why such importance was attached to silence in the desert. 'Silence not only prevented one from using language in a harmful way but also provided the fertile ground out of which words of power could grow and through which words could bear fruit in lives of holiness.'[7] The desert fathers and mothers offer invaluable insight for spiritual directors as to the part silence plays in our relationship with God. 'Go to your cell and your cell will teach you everything' was the advice given to an eager young man seeking to live close to God.[8] He did not find this easy advice to follow and did not even understand it at first. He wanted something to do. Alone in his cell he was first bored, then distracted, then as the monsters in his mind began to have a field day, he was afraid. The point was that this was the only way to find freedom from the endless conversations that go on in our heads so that we may know ourselves and come to know God. We cannot hear above the noise of our own thoughts and the intrusion of the many distractions the world offers that prevent us listening inwardly. Good directors in the modern context will help directees pay attention to their circumstances and the issues thrown up by them. In the desert context, silence and solitude focused attention on particular moral, ascetical and psychological questions. Today the questions might have more to do with a context where noise and lack of space prevail rather than silence and solitude. The desert fathers and mothers learned what it meant to stand before God without needing to justify or condemn themselves and to know they were loved. The desert is a place of stripping, of the cleansing of the human soul, and most people who pay attention to the Holy Spirit in their lives via spiritual direction will at some point find themselves in that place. It is the place where we may be released from our false, illusory selves and grow towards free and humble trust in God, which enables us to be the greater selves we are created to be. We find that we are forced to wait, that God seems silent and that we are reduced to passivity. At such times we will need the faithful companionship of another who is willing to wait with us, perhaps occasionally in literal silence and not be phased by it. The desert fathers also help us understand the importance of a single verse of Scripture and the impact it may have upon us. The best known desert father is St Antony of Egypt, who in 270, as a rich young man of 18, had been mulling over the words of Jesus to the rich ruler. When he went to church and heard the Gospel of the day read aloud it turned his life around. The passage was Mark 10.21: 'go, sell what you own, and give the money to the poor, and you will have treasure in heaven; then come, follow me.' Antony took the words literally and first lived a life of poverty, manual labour and prayer in his home village. He also put himself under the direction of an older man. Fifteen years later he went into the desert to live the life of a hermit, where his reputation for wisdom and holiness grew. Eventually after many years in solitude other desert dwellers begged him to come out of his cell and be their guide.

For Antony, Mark 10.21 became the watchword for his life. It was his *cantus firmus* and shaped his entire future. It is interesting that this particular verse has shaped the lives of other significant individuals in the history of the Church, notably St Francis, and it is also the verse that gives rise to many discussions on how far we should interpret certain parts of Scripture literally. For many people it is a single verse of Scripture that speaks to them above all others and often hits them with life-changing consequences. They will turn to other parts of the Bible but it is this one verse or passage that acts as the rudder of their lives, directing them in the way God is calling them to go. It may be a more general saying but still one that determines a person's values. I had a friend whose watchword was 'walk in the light' – she sought to measure all decisions by this phrase. Directors may be instrumental in reminding directees of a time in their lives when a verse seemed to be especially helpful, taking them back to such clarity when their situation grows difficult or opaque. At other times they may sense that it is important to bring different biblical themes to bear on choices and decisions so that fixation with a single verse does not limit further insight.

The desert fathers and mothers did not quote Scripture directly very often, but they patterned their own lives on it and were saturated with it. They may not have owned many copies of the Bible but it was everywhere: on their lips as they prayed, in conversations between abbas and their disciples, during their battles with demons and in encounters with locals, both saints and sinners. Burton-Christie notes that its use was 'almost always practical, spontaneous, informal and full of vitality' – which could be read as a blueprint for every spiritual director.[9] The idea of feeding on Scripture was familiar to these men and women, and ruminating was part of the process by which they learned to 'put on' Christ (Rom. 13.14; cf. Col. 3.12). For them the word of God and the life of the believer were inseparable, and they saw it as imperative that they submit to its commands. St Basil of Caesarea, for example, one of the early leaders of the monastic life that emerged from the desert, taught that every word and action must be checked against the witness of Scripture. Actions included simple everyday things like eating and sleeping as well as the complex motives of the human heart. This practical approach to Scripture meant that it sometimes became a foil to help the monks overcome self-deception, sometimes it was a mirror in which they faced their motives and sometimes a guide to their behaviour.

The desert fathers and mothers eventually died out but the tradition of solitary charismatic persons living on the edge of society continued in the Christian East, while monasticism spread to both East and West. Solitaries and monastic communities have had an important influence on the ministry of spiritual direction. A close personal relationship between a spiritual father or elder and his child in God is central to Eastern Christianity, and the role of spiritual direction is key to the relationship. It has remained a hidden tradition but it has gone on continuously. Bishop Kallistos Ware goes so far as to say that there has been an invisible apostolic succession existing on a charismatic level, which has operated alongside the visible official apostolic succession of bishops within the life of the Church.[10]

Like John the Baptist living in the liminal place between Old and New Testaments, the desert fathers and mothers bore witness to the living Word. It is interesting to notice that whenever and wherever the Church has experienced renewal, interest in these enigmatic characters and their practices has also revived.

Benedictine spirituality

Like the desert fathers and mothers, St Benedict, himself a desert dweller, understood the importance of listening. 'Listen carefully, my son, to the master's instructions, and attend to them with the ear of your heart' are the opening words of *The Rule of Benedict*.[11]

There is an emphasis in Benedictine spirituality on constant returning to the divine presence. Everything in the daily routine of a Benedictine is directed towards this attentiveness. It is cultivated through the liturgy, silence and reading the Scriptures.

It is the Benedictine tradition that has honed and handed on the practice of slow, meditative reading of Scripture known as *lectio divina*, or sacred reading. John Cassian brought this method to the West from the early monastic movement he had encountered in the East in the early fifth century, and it became firmly established as a way to enable Scripture to penetrate deeply into the human heart and 'Let the word of Christ dwell in you richly' (Col. 3.16).

It has been described in many ways. Just as a cow chewing its cud after eating a quantity of grass slowly and leisurely extracts all the goodness, so we ruminate on Scripture. 'O taste and see that the LORD is good' (Ps. 34.8). Others prefer the image of a boiled sweet, Baron von Hügel likening the process to 'letting a very slowly dissolving lozenge melt imperceptibly in your mouth'.[12] Some may prefer to imagine sampling fine wine. Eugene Peterson remarks that Spirit-sourced writing – that is, Scripture – requires spiritual reading, a reading that honours words as holy words, 'words as a basic means of forming an intricate web of relationships between God and the human, between all things visible and invisible'.[13] The Benedictine monk and spiritual writer David Foster urges his readers to read the Scriptures as if Jesus himself is there reading to us and our task is simply to listen.[14] This means that we place ourselves in a position whereby Scripture can do something to us and we are submitting to its agenda rather than imposing our own on it. This is a very import-ant point. In spiritual direction neither director nor directee is 'in charge'. Even though we insist that this time is for directees to explore their relationship with God, at every moment both director and directee are submitting to the Holy Spirit. Returning to a focus on what Scripture is saying enables this precious time to be given over to God. Learning to do this through slow, meditative *lectio* enables this to happen more often in the rest of life so that the power of God's word becomes transformative. *Lectio* involves slow reading because we are going at God's pace and most of us will have to learn this art because our culture is so much more at home with speed reading. *Lectio divina* has four parts to it, and it would not be difficult for a director to introduce the technique to a directee by doing it together.

Reading

The first part is the reading itself, *lectio*, where we choose a passage and read it through slowly two or three times. It may be helpful to read it aloud even if alone, savouring the words and noticing when we feel drawn to a particular word or phrase. We may repeat that word or phrase to ourselves to help it sink in. It is the business of getting the Scriptures from the head to the heart that is so core to living the Scriptures, rather than merely assenting to them intellectually. Only then can we be shaped by Scripture rather than by the prevailing culture or our own desires and ideas. As the Benedictine Abbot Marmion said, 'We read under the eye of God until the heart is touched and leaps to flame.'[15] When we have settled on one section of the reading we then stay with that part.

Meditation

Then the second part, that of meditation, *meditatio*, begins. Meditation is not, as some Christians fear, a way of emptying the mind or drifting off into a state of oblivion. It has clear biblical precedents that suggest that there has always been an issue around God's word sinking into human hearts. The opening of our minds and hearts are required for meditation as we 'Listen . . . with the ear of your heart', to quote again from the beginning of *The Rule of Benedict*. In the Scriptures, meditation is associated with the mouth, which chimes in well with the picture of the cow chewing its cud above. Thus 'The mouth of the righteous brings forth wisdom' (Prov. 10.31), while the psalmist regards God's word as containing a honey-like sweetness (Ps. 119.103).[16] It is important to notice that we are not simply trying to 'get' the meaning of the text by thinking hard. Its meaning may unfold gradually as we go on returning to the same text at other times. Further passages of Scripture may suggest themselves as shedding light on the one to hand, and in fact meditation is a good way to help us link different parts of the Bible in our thoughts and imaginations. It also helps to prevent mental wool-gathering if we try to relate one Scripture to another and the text as a whole to different events and issues in our lives. This helps to keep the meditation real and relevant and takes away the temptation to drift as we seek connections. For the people of the Old Testament the heart was first and foremost the seat of the will and of the affections, the place of discernment and the source of our intentions. It was like the engine room of the entire person. Although *lectio* uses the mind to think, it also has a place for feelings, in such a way that if we pay attention to them they too have things to tell us. The Holy Spirit is able to speak to us through our emotions, and indeed our felt response is a good way to find a path to the door of the heart (Heb. 4.12–16).

Prayer

Responding to the word of God to us personally leads naturally to prayer, *oratio*, the third part of *lectio divina*. The aim of *lectio* is to deepen our relationship with God, to let the word make its home in us so we will want to talk to the Lord about what we have heard. Jesus promised to come and make his home in us, but it is also true to say that we are being invited to make our home in God. 'How lovely is your dwelling place, O LORD of hosts!' The same psalm goes on to say 'Happy are those who live in your house', and the writer exclaims 'I would rather be a doorkeeper in the house of my God than live in the tents of wickedness' (Ps. 84.1, 4, 10). Jesus spoke of abiding in him and of his making his home in us. He said: 'Those who love me will keep my word, and my Father will love them, and we will come to them and make our home with them' (John 14.23). Earlier in the Gospel he had spoken about 'continuing in his word' where the word 'to continue' in the Greek can mean 'stay' or 'dwell'. Thus God's word is the source of our communion with the divine, expressed in and through prayer. As we meditate on the word we turn our thoughts into prayer to God, telling the Lord what is on our hearts and listening for the Spirit's response. There may be something to do, an attitude to attend to, someone to see, for God's words may come as comfort or challenge, rebuke or reassurance. We may be confident that however they come, God's words to us are words of life, and we can share all our deepest thoughts and feelings with our loving Lord. Our hopes, desires, sadness, confusion, disappointment, gratitude, rage or fear are all contained within God's loving caress. *Lectio* assures us that God speaks personally to us through Scripture without letting us privatize it.

Contemplation

Sometimes there is nothing to do but rest in God's love, and contemplation, *contemplatio*, is the fourth part of *lectio divina*. When we have said what we need to say, even if we know there is something to be done, it is important, first of all, simply to rest in God's presence at the end of meditating on the word. We may picture it as gazing on the Lord's loveliness, knowing that God gazes back at us and likes what is seen. It is something that cannot be hurried and should not be omitted. It involves 'waiting on God', and waiting takes time. We may or may not be aware that anything is happening at this point but we trust that God is working in the depths of our being. We can only do this if we believe God loves us unconditionally and delights in us so much that the living Word comes and makes a home in us. This may be where spiritual directors can work with directees on what they really believe about God, the images of God carried around perhaps unconsciously and the messages received about pleasing the deity. At any stage of *lectio*, however, they may be helpful in unpacking what has been going on and teasing out what God has been saying and what has not been said. As with all prayer, the process of review is important – another person listening in may help notice what has been happening, especially where there has been resistance or particular resonances that recur. Some people find it helpful to record their thoughts in these prayer times in a notebook or journal, which could be material for an appointment with a director.

Read, reflect, respond, rest – the order may get mixed up and we may not be sure whether we are praying or meditating, but that is less important than the process of letting the word of God take root in us and grow. David Foster comments in *Reading with God*:

> I like to think of a triangle linking myself, the Scriptures and God: I can read the Scriptures to develop a deeper understanding of God; I can find God using the Scriptures to help me to reach a better understanding of myself; and in my conversation with God, I can begin to get a clearer understanding of how he uses the Scriptures to address me and draw me to himself. Always the aim is to deepen my sense of friendship with him and commitment to him.[17]

Foster's words are an echo of a much earlier prayer by St Augustine:

> All shall be Amen and Alleluia.
> We shall rest and we shall see,
> We shall see and we shall know,
> We shall know and we shall love,
> We shall love and we shall praise.
> Behold our end which is no end.[18]

The practice of *lectio* is the best way I know to enable the Scriptures to get off the page and into my DNA. It allows the text to percolate through the consciousness so that it becomes part of everyday life. The connections are often startling and are not restricted to the actual time of *lectio* but come and surprise us when we least expect them. At a time of deep loss, for example, I happened on the words from Exodus 33.14: 'My presence will go with you, and I will give you rest.' Those words and my reflections on them sustained me for many days. A spiritual director could be important in helping us to learn how to read the Scriptures in a meditative way so that we are better placed to hear God speaking through them. We are bombarded with words at every turn and there are so many voices clamouring for our attention. We have learned to scan texts quickly for the information we need, to gut books for academic study, skim-read for the basic facts, rip through novels to get the gist of the story, block out thousands of words we don't need to see. Speed-reading is of the essence. However can we hope to read Scripture in such a way that we can expect to hear God's still small voice? We need to learn the art of slow reading so we do not miss the word of life the Scriptures offer us. Part of this lost art revolves around our expectations. What do we expect to find when we open the Scriptures? I and many others have found that having a spiritual director is one way to raise expectations that God has a personal word for me when I open the Scriptures, and that when there seems to be a disconnect between the Scriptures and life, talking things through with a director has helped me reconnect the two.

Ignatian prayer

Many spiritual directors are trained exclusively in Ignatian prayer and approach spiritual direction out of this tradition. Following the

Second Vatican Council the Jesuit Order began to offer retreats and training in retreat-giving to lay people, including non-Catholics. The influence of centres such as St Beuno's Jesuit Spirituality Centre in North Wales has led to the availability of Ignatian trained directors throughout the UK.

When people hear the words 'Ignatian prayer' they often assume it is all about praying with the imagination, but Ignatius taught his disciples to pray in many different ways. He himself was influenced by various strands of the Christian tradition, for example Benedictines, Dominicans, Carthusians and Franciscans. His favourite book was the *Imitatio Christi* of Thomas à Kempis, which came out of the *Devotio moderna*, a lay movement originating in Holland in the late fourteenth century that sought to revive and deepen the spiritual life.

It is Ignatius' method of approaching Scripture with the imagination to contemplate the scenes and encounter Jesus, however, that is typical of the contemporary interest in his spirituality. He encouraged his disciples to contemplate, via the imagination, an event in the life of Jesus because he understood that our imaginations are linked to our deepest feelings and values, which in turn influence our choices and decisions. For Ignatius, the imagination as well as the mind was important for discerning the truth, for both involved the rational. He also taught the importance of repetition of imaginative exercises so that the person praying could enter more deeply into the encounter with Jesus.

Ignatius was converted while convalescing at a monastery following injury in battle. He was overcome with boredom – all he had to read were romances of the period. He was then given two books: one on the lives of the saints – *The Golden Legend* by Jacobus de Voragine (1230–98) – and *The Life of Christ* by Ludolph of Saxony (*c*.1295–1378). It was as he read and contemplated the stories in these that he noticed how they affected his moods. On reading the romances he would think about them afterwards and very soon feel as desolate and empty as before. But when he read and contemplated the life of Jesus, the good feelings he experienced stayed with him for a long time after. This was the beginning of his great insight concerning the process he later called 'the discernment of spirits', which we might think of today as learning to sift our moods and feelings in order to follow Christ's way. As we proceed in the Christian life our whole being reacts to the direction of travel. If we are wholly directed towards God and God's will for us, our creative moods, feelings and actions will result in peace and joy and build up our faith, while the destructive ones will lead to turmoil and sadness and will undermine faith. Conversely, if the core of our being is turned away from God, then our destructive moods will comfort and console us while our creative moods will disturb and upset us. Ignatius referred to these two kinds of feelings as consolation and desolation. Those feelings and moods that draw us to God are consolation while those that cause us to turn away are desolation. Often these feelings surface as we pray with the Scriptures by entering into a Gospel scene and notice what is going on inside us.

Ignatius wrote his *Spiritual Exercises* as a manual to help his disciples pray. It sets out a number of different styles and methods. As those undertaking the exercises pray, they are confronted with the fundamental images of the gospel that challenge and enable transformation to take place. Scripture plays a central part in Ignatius' understanding of prayer. It is important to remember that he did not have all the critical tools at our disposal with regard to reading Scripture (which are of course both an aid and a hindrance to coming into contact with the text of the Bible). He died in 1556 when the Council of Trent had just started to meet. A man of his time, Ignatius was influenced by the Renaissance with its emphasis on learning and the desire to return to the sources. But he was not concerned with who wrote what, how or where, and was highly subjective in the way he expected the Bible to make its impact upon the reader, drawing freely on his own experiences. He expected people to use their senses to help them experience Christ as fully as possible, which accounts for his attention to what to us might seem peripheral matters, such as the environment in which we pray, our bodily posture and even the kind of food we eat – he knew these things can affect our capacity to pray. Ignatius set out a structure for prayer that involved preparatory exercises and 'preludes' to prayer to help set the scene, and was supremely practical in his approach. He was not a speculative theologian and preferred stories and images from the Scriptures to provide the focus for praying. The heart and the affections were central to his way of praying, though he did not neglect the intellect, which he also valued. Indeed he went back to school after his conversion in order to learn Latin so that he could read the Scriptures for himself. He carried a copy of the Gospels with the words of Jesus in red, so eager was he to meditate closely on the words uttered by the Lord.

The mantra often associated with Ignatian prayer is 'finding God in all things', and the principle rests on Ignatius' conviction that it is in the here and now that we will find God or not at all. The whole created world is the arena that mediates God and in which God is continually at work. Ignatius was not so naïve as to think there were not forces that militated against finding God, and demonstrated this most clearly in a very important 'meditation on the two standards' in his *Spiritual Exercises*. In this meditation everything is the scene of a great conflict between Christ and his kingdom on the one hand, and the forces of evil and the kingdom these represent on the other. Nothing is excluded from this conflict, and we must learn to discern and discriminate so that we may recognize the presence and action of God and choose which kingdom we will serve.

Ignatius was interested in helping people to pray so that they could be involved in the world more fully. Prayer and life must therefore be fully integrated. Besides the imaginative prayer described here, the other vital tool in the *Spiritual Exercises* designed to help us discern God in our lives is the 'Examen of consciousness' or 'review of the day'. This is a simple way of learning to look for God's presence in our daily lives and so find 'God in all things'. It involves reflecting on the day that has just past, the events, encounters and conversations, but also our feelings and their underlying moods, noticing where God has been present and we have been aware of that presence, and where we have missed God or failed to respond. We invite the Holy Spirit to lead us in this exercise and help us pay attention. We might choose one particular feature from the day and pray around it. Ignatius is adamant that this is not an exercise in self-condemnation. We are to notice, not judge; to give thanks first and foremost and only then express sorrow for the times we have let our Lord down. At the end we look ahead to the next day and ask for whatever we need. Ignatius encouraged his disciples to talk to Jesus as they would a friend. While not an exercise that directly uses Scripture, the Examen will help us notice more in our ordinary lives the God we meet in the Bible and so connect the two together. It is a tool to help people reflect theologically on their lives and realize that God is indeed 'in all things'. In this way the exercise is very like spiritual direction itself.

Ignatian spirituality speaks clearly to people today who seek the benefits of spiritual direction. The combination of engaging with Scripture and reflecting on our lives in order to live more deeply out of God's will for us presents us with an invitation to become more fully awake at all times and not just in the moments we set aside for prayer. Ignatius' principle of flexibility and adaptation according to the needs of the individual mean that directees do not need to fear that their director will try to squeeze them into a mould, while Ignatius' insistence that we must let go of 'attachments' that prevent us living out of freedom is a particular challenge to a world mired in materialism and a preoccupation with self-image. His approach is also a helpful reminder on the role of the director, in that he was very clear that nothing should interfere in allowing 'the Creator to deal directly with the creature and the creature directly with his Creator and Lord'.[19] There are a number of contemporary writers who have made the *Spiritual Exercises* accessible to modern Christians. Perhaps the best known is Gerard Hughes, whose *God of Surprises* is already counted among the Christian classics.[20] There is also a much-used and Scripture-based online resource designed to help people 'pray as they go' – see <www.sacredspace.ie>.

Ignatius originally intended his *Spiritual Exercises* to be under-taken during a 30-day retreat, but from the beginning he made an important concession in what is known as the 'nineteenth annotation', which reads: 'Make even extraordinary adaptations in direction for persons in extraordinary circumstances.' This allows people to do the *Spiritual Exercises* and pray with Scripture in the midst of daily life.

Evangelical spirituality

The principle of applying the Scriptures to daily life is fundamental to evangelical spirituality and it is perhaps not surprising that many evangelicals have found themselves at home with Ignatian-style prayer as described above. Although spiritual direction as described here is not integral to evangelical Christianity, there are many evangelicals today who have found it beneficial to have a spiritual director and have discovered that there are similarities between this ministry and their own emphasis on prayer, witness and spiritual growth. Many young people who have come to faith within the evangelical fold will have been assigned an older Christian with whom to pray or read the Bible, and the idea of a Paul–Timothy relationship is a familiar one. One-to-one discipling has always had a place in encouraging new Christians to put down roots in four classic areas: prayer, Bible reading, fellowship and evangelism. The expectation is that growth is an integral part of the Christian life and that people need help to keep going in their faith. As evangelicalism has broadened and discovered some of the riches of the wider Christian tradition, evangelicals have found ways to integrate their love of the Scriptures and stress on the Lordship of Christ in a person's life, using the practice of spiritual direction along with retreats and a commitment to the spiritual disciplines of solitude and silence. In its turn, the evangelical insistence on the supreme value and authority of Scripture is an important contribution to the spirituality debate, providing it with substance and identity. The habit of learning Bible verses has always been a key aspect of discipleship in evangelical spirituality, so that Christians carry within them the Scriptures they revere. There are other key features of this tradition that often crop up in direction as issues for people seeking to deepen their faith. For example, the centrality of the cross, also prominent in Ignatian spirituality, shows us the true character of a God who loves us unconditionally.[21] We do not have to earn God's approval, indeed we cannot do so. Salvation is a gift of grace, not of works (Eph. 2.8–9). God is our heavenly father who delights to pour out grace upon God's beloved children, rather than a fierce judge who must be appeased by fearful humans. The priesthood of all believers, a central tenet of the Reformation, is a reminder of the dignity of each person's experience of God and that each one is able to come into the presence of the living Lord and remain there; it is also a useful reminder to any directors who may harbour delusions about their importance to directees' personal experience of God. Another feature of evangelical faith is the reality of assurance. A much-quoted passage is Paul's confidence in Romans 8.38–39 that nothing in the whole of creation can separate us from the love of God in Christ. Our relationship with God is direct, personal and devotional. Evangelicals are also aware of the frailties of human nature and that Christian maturity does not come about without effort and sometimes real struggle. Spiritual growth is understood in terms of growth in holiness.[22] The Puritan strand of evangelicalism stressed this aspect of spiritual life, which offers many vital insights into areas of resistance that writers on spiritual

direction discuss.[23] Finally, evangelicalism, although stressing personal conversion and displaying a tendency towards individualism,
is at its core an outward-looking faith. Social action has been a driving force in evangelicalism, for our relationship with Jesus Christ is
not simply for our personal delectation but for the sake of the kingdom of God. Prayer and social action therefore go together and no
one in this tradition would be content to withdraw into a spiritual
vacuum that failed to recognize that a relationship with God has
consequences for us in the world.

Anglican spiritual direction

Anglican spirituality has grown and developed from the deep roots of
the Christian Church in the British Isles, even though it was the late
sixteenth and early seventeenth centuries when it became embedded
in the culture. Spiritual direction in the Anglican tradition has
tended to be regarded as an aspect of pastoral care exercised by the
ordained and has operated on two models: an educational one that
encompasses the whole person, and the model of the shepherd tend-
ing his flock. In both cases they have largely been embodied in the
clergy, with some notable exceptions.

The vision of Archbishop Cranmer in the sixteenth century was
for everyone to have access to the Bible in their own language and
to be able to come to God in prayer without any intermediary. Prayer
and spirituality had become inaccessible for ordinary people, so from
now on they were to hear the Scriptures read twice a day in church
when the priest rang the bell to summon them to prayer. Cranmer
condensed the monastic hours into morning and evening prayer,
which he envisaged being prayed by all Christians each day. The Book
of Common Prayer is not directly concerned with matters of spiritual direction, although when the minister read the Exhortation to
come to communion the day before it was celebrated, he was to offer
'ghostly counsel and advice' by means of the ministry of God's holy
word to anyone who was in need of 'comfort or counsel'.

A group of clergy in the late sixteenth and seventeenth centuries
known as the Caroline Divines, who included Lancelot Andrewes,
George Herbert, John Donne and Jeremy Taylor, took personal spiritual guidance as a *sine qua non* of Christian living. And, of course,
they lived and breathed the Scriptures and the Book of Common

Prayer, itself saturated with the Scriptures, so that to separate the Bible from life would have been inconceivable. Writing to his clergy in his diocese of Down and Connor, Jeremy Taylor exhorted them:

> to a conversation with their minister in spiritual things, to an enquiry concerning all parts of their duty; for by preaching and catechizing and private intercourse all the needs of the soul can best be served; but by preaching alone they cannot.[24]

In *A Priest to the Temple, Or, The Country Parson*, the poet and parson George Herbert described the parson as one 'who hath thoroughly digested all the points of consolation', and we may assume these would be as grounded in the Scriptures as Herbert's poetry.[25]

The Book of Common Prayer was and continues to be a particular way of praying the Scriptures and so formed the basis of all direction offered within this tradition. It was a lay spirituality and covered the whole of life from cradle to grave, providing prayers concerning everyday life – for rain, harvest, peace, those at sea, birth, marriage and death.

As someone brought up on extempore prayer and Bible notes written freshly every few months by numerous anonymous authors, the idea of a daily-office style of prayer was foreign to me. But I discovered, like so many others, that learning to use a daily office was like a homecoming. There was a great difference between repetition and vain repetition. Many people in spiritual direction who have hit a dryness in prayer have found, paradoxically, that using a regular daily office has kept them grounded and enabled them to reconnect with God. Others who have struggled for years with making a regular space for prayer and Bible reading have been helped by the structure of a daily office. Far from offering people something that appears rigid, restricting, boring or repetitious, the suggestion that they join with others around the globe in faithfully repeating well-chosen words has enlivened faith and restored perspective. Praying an office is not about repeating words parrot-fashion in a disengaged state of mind but allowing them to sink deeply into the whole of one's being in a similar way to the practice of *lectio divina*. The Book of Common Prayer is almost wholly words of Scripture rearranged in a particular way. It is accompanied by the lectionary, set Bible readings and Psalms for every day of the year. Today the Revised Common Lectionary means that Christians of different traditions are following the same pattern of readings throughout the year. Cranmer arranged the Psalter so that the whole of it was said every month and the readings from the Old Testament were so arranged that it was read through once each year and the New Testament twice. Liturgical revision has brought changes but has not lost sight of the principle of praying words based in the Scriptures. Moreover there is variety within the familiar pattern according to the Church's year, so that we are enabled to dwell in the seasons through Scriptures that help us engage with them more deeply than we could otherwise.

There are many alternative daily offices around today. One that many people are finding helpful is that of the Northumbria Community. It is simple, brief and full of Scripture. People who would never dream of aligning themselves with liturgical worship have found it to be an anchor in the storm and water in the desert places. When life is chaotic we need a way of finding a rhythm that will hold us. Many of our churches do not do this, nor are they able to acknowledge that people are in different places mentally and emotionally when they come to church. The Book of Common Prayer, with its focus on the Psalms, speaks eloquently to this situation. In the Psalms we find the whole of life, every conceivable emotion. The Psalms assure us that it is all right to rage at God, to ask God 'Why?', to weep before God as well as rejoice and celebrate God's loving kindness. They even show us that we can pour out our vindictive feelings in God's hearing. If we are not experiencing the emotion being expressed in the Psalm we are saying together, we may be sure someone else in the gathering is – and it may be us next time. The daily office thus sets us free from the modern cult of individualism and roots us in a larger corporate tradition. It helps us mature as we realize we do not have to experience a high every time we pray, for it is much more to do with obedience, stability and the slow but sure conversion of the whole person towards God. Wise spiritual directors will always have this tool at their disposal to help those struggling to pray. And as with Ignatian prayer, there are numerous resources online to help busy people connect with others by way of a daily office.[26]

In the nineteenth century the Oxford Movement fostered the ministry of spiritual direction through its key figures, who included Edward Pusey, John Keble and John Henry Newman. Often it is in their correspondence that we see their regard for offering spiritual counsel to others, but it is in the twentieth century that we find one of the most influential figures where spiritual direction is concerned. Evelyn Underhill was a lay woman rather than a clergyman, and was described as 'the spiritual director of her generation'. As a retreat director, spiritual guide and writer on the spiritual life she influenced many by her wisdom and encouragement. She was adamant that what people wanted was God and that what was at stake was the spiritual health of the Church. Underhill wrote to the Archbishop of Canterbury prior to the 1930 Lambeth Conference to urge the assembled bishops to call the clergy to a life of prayer, because, she said:

> We look to the church to give us an experience of God, Mystery, Holiness, Prayer, which shall lift us to contact with the supernatural world – minister Eternal Life ... God is the interesting thing about religion and people are hungry for God. But only a priest whose life is soaked in prayer, sacrifice and love, can by his own spirit of adoring worship help us to apprehend him.[27]

Her comments are especially interesting in the light of the contemporary disaffection with the Church in general and concurrent hunger for spirituality. As a director herself, Underhill listened deeply, enabling people to connect their lives with God, and in her retreats she drew heavily on the Bible and the Christian writers and teachers of prayer down the ages, to ground this connection in the Christian tradition.

Models across the traditions

Not all traditions have been covered here and there are other models of spiritual direction that are more general and less tied to a particular spirituality or tradition. It is probably no accident that the crossing of denominational and other boundaries has led to much greater common ground in modelling good practice in spiritual direction. The models discussed here reinforce this approach, and in the remaining section the choice will be determined by images found in Scripture.

In *Holy Listening*, Margaret Guenther takes three biblical images and builds them into models of spiritual direction, all of which resonate with the contemporary world and have the advantage of not being the preserve of a particular ecclesiastical tradition.[28]

Midwife

The first is the director as midwife, a model based on the parallels between giving birth physically and spiritual birth and rebirth. This takes us directly to John 3, where Jesus himself states the necessity of spiritual rebirth. Whether we think in terms of an initial conversion experience or the ongoing work of the Holy Spirit bringing new life to birth within us, we are firmly in the realm of what is happening in spiritual direction. The image of the midwife is also helpful in other ways. We are taken back to the Old Testament as well as the Gospels and Epistles, for there at the beginning of the Exodus narrative are two midwives, Shiphrah and Puah, who were prepared to disobey the Pharaoh because they feared God, and so enabled the new life of the Israelite baby boys to continue (Exod. 1.15–21). There are a number of Bible stories about old women giving birth that can be read spiritually and help to enlarge our understanding of the work of the Spirit within us. Guenther points out that the midwife does things *with* the mother-to-be rather than *to* her. She works from the start to establish a relationship of trust, one where no question is out of order or considered stupid; she is comfortable with the questioning and uncertainty that often goes with early pregnancy, as with the beginnings of a new relationship with God; she is present through all the stages of giving birth, even when there is nothing apparently happening, at least on the surface; she has learned to watch and wait with patience and encourages the mother-to-be to persevere. The Spirit may be groaning deep down in the person's inner being and such struggle cannot be bypassed (Rom. 8.26). The midwife assists at what is a natural event and relies on skills that do not suggest that her charge is a patient but someone who is involved in a natural process. So it is with the spiritual director, who should not be confused with a counsellor or therapist but is someone working alongside another in the spiritual realm. It is very important that we know not to try to make it all better but to be there ready to assist if and when necessary. Finally the midwife shares in the joy of a safe delivery just as a spiritual director rejoices at moments of God's rich blessings in a human life.

Hospitality

Guenther's second model is that of hospitality, and she begins her reflections with the story from Genesis 18 where Abraham welcomed three strangers to his tent. The three travellers were in need of rest and refreshment. Abraham's tent was on their route and he had what they required and offered it gladly. There were very few choices open to such travellers as to places to stay, and like all travellers they could not simply keep on going without stopping. Today's seekers of spiritual refreshment have far more choices but will also have needs. They may have only travelled a short car journey to see their director, but inwardly they may well have come a great distance and still have far to go before they reach home. It may be the case that the person before us simply needs to pause, draw breath and find some refreshment for the journey and then move on. For some people a spiritual cleanup is necessary and directors find themselves in the role of confessor. Like good hosts, directors make themselves available to the needs of their guests, listen and then put themselves out of the way. By making space they give the impression of having all the time in the world.

'Do not neglect to show hospitality to strangers, for by doing that some have entertained angels without knowing it', urges the letter to the Hebrews (Heb. 13.2). We think we know x or y and then when we make space discover there is so much more to them. Like Abraham we discover that we are offering a mysterious ministry.

Teacher

As for Guenther's third model, that of teacher, there are over 40 references to Jesus as teacher in the Gospels, and of course it was observed early on that he taught with authority (Matt. 7.29; Mark 1.22; Luke 4.32). The teacher model may be the most important one to recover in our own time, when so few have any Christian foundations on which to build. The letter of James, however, warns that the office of teacher is a dangerous one, for 'we who teach will be judged with greater strictness' (James 3.1). 'Teacher' is a loving form of address but is respectful at the same time.

Among the qualities of good teachers are that of understanding their pupils' limits, encouraging them to ask their own questions, wanting them to grow into maturity and able to evaluate progress. A good teacher encourages play and enjoyment in learning. We are apt to make heavy weather of prayer, so assuring people that our relationship with God can be joyful and pure delight is invaluable. A good teacher gives homework, which may not at first sight seem very congenial to adults looking for God, not lists of things to do. What this could mean in spiritual direction might be to do with giving directees something new to think about; a new way of seeing that they could practise in daily life; a new approach to try in prayer. It will frequently mean referring them back to the Scriptures and encouraging them to meditate on them. Good teachers never stop learning themselves and all the great spiritual writers and teachers on direction are very clear that all the knowledge in the world is useless if a director has no personal experience of God and God's ways.

From these models it is clear what spiritual direction is not. It is not one Christian telling another Christian what to do, and it is not an attempt to clone Christians in a spiritual director's own image. It is very important that spiritual directors do not try to make others fit either their own experience or expectations. They have a crucial role as facilitators, guides and companions, but the integrity of those they direct remains paramount.

Gardeners, doctors and intercessors

Other models rooted in Scripture include the gardener, the doctor and the intercessor (I shall discuss that of the friend in the next section). Each highlights an aspect of spiritual direction that needs to be borne in mind by all who participate in direction. The image of the gardener is one that is applied to God in Scripture, and the image of the garden itself is a recurring one. Paul wrote in 1 Corinthians of how 'I planted, Apollos watered, but God gave the growth' (1 Cor. 3.6). Other Christian writers have taken up this theme, especially St Teresa of Ávila, who wrote a famous description of prayer as akin to watering a garden. Different methods of watering require greater or lesser effort, which she likens to different kinds of prayer.[29] Jesus referred to himself as the Vine and his father as the gardener. We are the branches who must abide in him if we are to bear fruit and flourish. His father will prune the fruit-bearing branches – a painful but necessary exercise if we are to continue to grow healthily. Shifting the image (while staying with agriculture), it is important to remember that we are 'God's field' (1 Cor. 3.9) and that the seed within us grows secretly by God's hand. This may be helpful for a bemused director who is in need of patience or encouragement to go on watering the ground. St Madeleine Sophie, the French founder of the Society of the Sacred Heart, warned:

> [He] wants to make use of us, certainly, but only as instruments and not as movers. Let us allow him to act. Let us be no more than a gardener who cultivates the soil; he turns it over and pulls out the weeds; but once the seed has been sown he has no more to do than to water it and to drive away the insects or other enemies of the plant.[30]

The Scriptures are full of helpful material for reflection on this theme, not least in those many parables of Jesus that deal with growing things, such as the sower, the wheat and the tares, references to the lilies of the field and so on. The fruit of the Spirit is another New Testament theme to ponder in prayer with the help of a spiritual director.

The image of the doctor again finds its source in God who is the Great Physician. However much we may wish to see ourselves as tenders of souls, it is God who brings about healing in our lives and makes us whole. The spiritual director as doctor was the dominant model in the Christian East from the fourth century onwards. Athanasius described St Antony as 'a doctor given by God to Egypt'.[31] Confession to a spiritual father was seen in therapeutic rather than legalistic terms, as was the case in the Celtic tradition. Dom John Chapman, an influential spiritual director in the late nineteenth and early twentieth centuries, described the director as a nurse rather than a doctor, saying:

> he should confine himself to the task of teaching his penitents how to walk alone and unaided. That done, he should retire into the background; only emerging on rare occasions when unusual circumstances or some particular crisis called for his assistance.[32]

Jesus' healing ministry in the Gospels provides much material for meditation on this theme – for example, who he healed, what he said to the sick person and what he said about sickness.

The image of intercessor is not by any means restricted to spiritual directors, but it is a useful reminder that those who are coming to talk to us need our prayers and that praying for those entrusted to our care is an integral part of spiritual direction. Indeed our prayers are probably more important than anything we might say. One visitor to Mount Athos asked an elder: 'May I write to you sometimes to ask for advice?' The monk replied 'No. But I will pray for you.' The visitor was downcast but another monk said to him: 'You ought to be very happy that the geronta promised to pray for you; he doesn't say that to everyone. His advice is good; but his prayers are far, far better.'[33] Over and over again the apostle Paul asked those he had brought to spiritual new birth to pray for him, and his letters are in turn full of his own prayers for them. These prayers bear much reflection for any desiring more of God for themselves. Committing to pray for those we direct helps us stay in touch in the intervening weeks – and perhaps months – between visits, and as we bring them before God, God is able to help us learn to see them as God sees them. The Holy Spirit may also use our intercessions to bring to light things that need attention when we next meet. Directees in turn should pray for those who direct them, not least that they will be given wisdom. I have found it a humbling experience to receive a note of encouragement from a spiritual director ending with a request for my prayers. Paul shared the burdens of those in his spiritual care, showing his willingness both to share and identify himself with them: 'Who is weak, and I am not weak? Who is made to stumble, and I am not indignant?' (2 Cor. 11.29).

Friendship

In some ways the model of friendship underlies all the other models mentioned so far, although it requires some qualifications in this context.[34] Friends introduce one another to new things and places, a fresh way of seeing something, a word of encouragement and the occasional challenge. They make space for us and let us be ourselves. Friends stick with each other through thick and thin and do not run away when one is struggling, bowed down or behaving badly. A good friend bears our burdens with us. Friendship is an important dimension to recall when spiritual direction is beset by a false professionalism that threatens its human and informal nature. It is important to judge directors more by their prayerfulness and openness to the Spirit than by their qualifications. 'When you find a good person, beat a path to their door', said one of the early Church Fathers – even today word of mouth is often still the best way to locate a good director. God invites us to friendship, and there is an element of spiritual direction that is based on friendship, even though it may be less than mutual to be effective. Between director and directee there is a sense of solidarity and shared love within the body of Christ. St Aelred, a Cistercian monk who lived in the twelfth century, wrote about friendship in ways that may be applied directly to the spiritual direction setting: 'Here we are, you and I and I hope, a third, Christ, in our midst.'[35] He was convinced that loving other human beings does not keep us from loving God but in fact enables us to grow in the love of God. Furthermore, friendship is a symbol of our life in the Trinity, and reflection on the relationship between the Father, Son and Holy Spirit leads us into the freedom to trust others who share our spiritual journey with us.

Aelred drew his picture of friendship from John's Gospel, where Jesus called his disciples friends. We get a sense of the kind of friendship meant in this context from the Celtic tradition of soul friend, the *anam chara*. They were spiritual guides and directors of souls but it was clearly a one-sided affair. The Celtic saying, 'A person without a soul friend is like a body without a head', is not describing non-directive soul making. In pre-Christian times the druids had acted as spiritual guides to Irish chieftains and the model was copied within the emerging Christian communities. Celtic soul friends doled out penances which, while designed to restore the penitent to wholeness by fitting the penance to the misdemeanour (as with the doctor model), were often extremely harsh. One thinks of the apostle Paul wrestling with his treatment of the Corinthians (2 Cor. 1—2). When thinking of spiritual direction in terms of friendship there needs to be an element of distance maintained on the part of the director. Other models provide help with this.

Alternative models of direction

It is instructive to consider the role of certain Bible characters in the light of qualities desirable in a director or the way direction is given. Paul, for example, had an itinerant ministry of preaching but the New Testament contains a number of his letters in which much spiritual direction is given both to individuals, like Timothy, and whole congregations, as at Corinth, Thessalonica and Philippi. Paul wrote his letters to build up his congregations. He frequently referred to the Scriptures, which for him were the Old Testament. He wrote to expand the knowledge and experience of young Christians and inspire in them the desire to know more of God and to help them work out how in various situations they should live as followers of Christ.

Spiritual direction by correspondence is a long-standing method of guiding other Christians. From St Augustine to Martin Luther, St Bernard to John Keble, many well-known Christian teachers and leaders have found time to write to individuals to offer spiritual counsel and guidance. Many other unknown pastors and teachers have also practised this invaluable ministry. Until quite recently these writers could assume a working knowledge of Scripture on the part of those to whom they wrote, which is not always the case today. Emails, Tweets and blogs are now more likely choices for communication, and there is evidence that Scripture continues to play a prominent part. It certainly offers a powerful means of enabling the words of the Bible to make an impact in a 'pray-as-you-go' society. Those with a good knowledge of the Bible could include Scripture references and encourage recipients to look them up in a Bible app and then respond in various ways with action, reflection or comment.

8

Prayer and praying

Learning to pray

The practice of prayer lies at the heart of spiritual direction. Prayer is focused on our relationship with God. It is the basic tool of communication in that relationship and both Scripture and our experience feed into it. The scriptural dimension means that prayer is ever ancient while our experience means it is ever new. At its simplest prayer is conversation with God, and as with every conversation, the character and personality of the participants shapes its tone and content. There is, first of all, the character of God whom we address in prayer, and what we understand and believe that character to be is crucial to how we pray. But there is also the human factor in prayer. Few people are taught how to pray and today very few adults will have learned simple prayers at their mother's knee or attended Sunday School, where they would have learned some basic ways of praying and committed a few prayers to memory. Most people simply copy what they see others doing and, if they are fortunate, may gain some insight through a Lent course or a book from the church bookstall. It is not surprising that one of the main reasons people seek a spiritual director is a sense of dissatisfaction with their prayer life. This should be viewed as a very good reason for turning to spiritual direction, and directors need to be valued by the Church for the help they supply to so many Christians on this front. Where prayer is concerned, frustration, a sense of failure or simply bafflement prevents many Christians from experiencing a sense of the reality of God in their lives. Prayer is a monologue for many people, a list of petitions or a steady stream of conscious thought directed towards God in the hope they will be heard. We talk and God listens. Indeed God does listen, graciously and lovingly. But this is not what we encounter in the Scriptures concerning prayer. For

100

the apostle Paul, prayer is a perpetual spring flowing out of the deep well of salvation. Prayer is so much more than we can imagine or know, but the more we practise the deeper we are invited to partake of its riches. It is possible for prayer to become an all-involving way of life.

Sustained by Scripture

The Bible and prayer have been regarded as fundamental to sustaining the Christian life in all the major traditions of Christian spirituality. It is therefore natural to expect that they will be at the heart of spiritual direction. The Bible, prayer and our experience are all related. Prayer that is life-giving is made up of human experience informed and nourished by the Scriptures. In prayer we are trying to allow the word of God to illuminate our experience. The Bible is also the chief source of nourishment for the spiritual life and so we need to find ways of dwelling in it so that we can digest it and grow. This does not mean trying to force meaning out of the portion of the Scriptures we have just read, but it could well mean living for a while with a piece of Scripture offered to us by a spiritual director who is open to the Spirit as we tell our story. It could also mean reading and praying through the Bible without demanding that it address directly our specific circumstances each time we open it. Christians believe that the Bible is a life-giving book that helps us to know God's presence in our lives and God's will and purpose for us. It assures us that God wants to communicate with us and demonstrates how others have responded in the past. It will teach us how to listen. As we seek to know the Lord's will better with the help of a spiritual director, God's word will play a central role in the relationship. It is the inspiration for prayer and the most trustworthy means of learning to listen to the voice of God in daily life.

Prayer as conversation with God

Prayer leads us to God in the way that conversation leads us to know a speaker better as we listen. Prayer that is grounded in the word of God will also lead to deeper living by that same word. It opens up the possibility of our whole lives being shaped by God's word. Henri Nouwen describes how prayer is a conversation, such that when we pray, God responds.[1] The divine response is clothed in the words of Scripture; so, for example, when the psalmist prays 'Answer me when I call, O God of my right! Be gracious to me, and hear my prayer' (Ps. 4.1), sometimes he hears God answer 'I am with you'. Sometimes in the night when the psalmist prays: 'Be pleased, O God, to deliver me. O LORD, make haste to help me!' (Ps. 70.1), he hears God answer: 'God is our refuge and strength, a very present help in trouble' (Ps. 46.1). And when the psalmist tells God how lonely and unloved he feels he often senses God's reassurance: 'His steadfast love endures for ever' (Ps. 118.2). This kind of praying echoes Scripture itself, for example when the author of Hebrews says 'he has said "I will never leave you or forsake you." So we can say with confidence, "The Lord is my helper; I will not be afraid. What can anyone do to me?"' (Heb. 13.5–6). Nouwen said that when he had prayed like this he would try to keep the word he had heard with him throughout the day, noting that mediated through the word, prayer became spiritual conversation with the One who knows and loves us. One of the underlying expectations of spiritual direction is that prayer can and should change as we change. We grow older, move house, suffer bereavement, start a family. We need to be able to pray as we are now, not as we were five years ago. We need to be able to recognize that we have changed and have courage to embrace that without feeling we are betraying what we used to be.

I have a friend who rings me up to chat and in the midst of speaking I find we are praying. My friend's words have widened from being addressed only to me to including God in the conversation. It is a very beautiful thing to experience and reminds me of how natural prayer should be. It is very easy to fence off prayer from the rest of life. The lines of communication with God are never closed, we say, yet in the same breath we talk about having a 'time of prayer'. By reflecting on daily experiences and where God may have been speaking to us, we are more likely to notice the Lord's active presence in our lives at other times.

Different kinds of praying

There are all kinds of prayers and all kinds of praying in the Christian faith. The traditional 'three ways' of purgation, illumination and union are not artificially imposed on the gospel but arise out of the very features of its content and message: repentance; life in the Spirit; perfection or sanctification.

We meet many prayerful encounters with God in the pages of the Bible. The Bible also forms us in prayer, for as we get to know its prayers and praying people we find that encounter character-forming. We discover the various forms of prayer – intercession, adoration, confession, thanksgiving – and we can make these prayers our own. We learn to know when to confess and when to intercede. We discover the vital and often missing ingredient of lament and learn to cry out before God on behalf of our own and others' pain. When our words run out we find the words of Scripture say what is on our heart. Perhaps the most important aspect of all regarding prayer in the Scriptures is the relational way it is expressed. 'When you pray,' said Jesus, 'say "Our Father"' (Luke 11.2). But there is so much more. Take Isaiah 43.1: 'But now thus says the LORD, he who created you, O Jacob, he who formed you, O Israel: Do not fear, for I have redeemed you; I have called you by name, you are mine.' Learning to hear these words as if spoken directly to us, we learn the heart of praying. To know God is calling us by name, that the Lord desires us and that we have no need to be afraid, means that we may pray in trust and hope. This opens up new avenues of prayer, such as enjoying being quiet in God's presence, knowing what it is like simply to 'be' as if we are in the presence of the one we love most and with whom we feel most secure. This is to know prayer as pure gift.

Prayer is task and gift at one and the same time. Nouwen believed that spiritual formation involves 'the practising of the paradox that prayer asks much effort but can only be received as a gift.'[2] We see prayer as gift and as task over and over again in the Scriptures, perhaps most clearly in the Psalms, which have been called the Church's prayer book.

Wants and needs

Peterson talks about the way the Scriptures introduce us to the three-personed God who challenges our sovereign self expressed in our holy wants, our holy needs and our holy feelings.[3] We bring our prayers shaped by our wants, needs and feelings, refusing to let God be God. When spiritual directors talk about resistance in direction, these are the barriers to which they refer – barriers that block out the voice of

God calling us to leave our needs, wants and feelings in order to be free. Let us be clear what we mean by this. We all have needs – legitimate needs – but often we mistake our felt needs for the real ones that would enable us to be truly children of God. Felt needs are often induced by the culture around us – we need to be comfortable, fulfilled, affirmed, successful. The Bible tells us we are usually looking in the wrong places for the wrong things. These needs that amount to our identity can only be found in knowing we are children of our heavenly father. We all have feelings and they are a necessary and legitimate part of our relationship with God. So often, however, we confuse the feelings that come with having a good time, being free from the stresses and strains of life, with knowing we are in the right place as far as God is concerned. Or we seek the feelings of what we imagine an exciting life in the Spirit ought to be, mistaking ecstasy or simply 'feeling good' for a deeper walk with God through the everyday moods we all experience. As for our wants, our culture has programmed us to want more and more and never be satisfied because the things we think we want are all designed to massage our ego and put self at the centre. When we listen to God's voice in Scripture and in prayer, we will never find such a message. On the contrary, Jesus said we must die to self if we want to follow him. A scary message indeed, so that 'Fear not' in Isaiah and in so many other places is a necessary precondition to letting go of our needs, wants and feelings and surrendering ourselves to God.

Spiritual direction is one way to find help in distinguishing between our real needs and our felt needs, our wants and our true desires. How do we discover these real needs and desires and the feelings that arise from knowing we are God's beloved? In the previous chapter I referred briefly to a story about a youth who wanted to join a monastery.[4] After persistent knocking he was finally admitted. 'At last,' he thought, 'I will be a monk.' But the abbot told him that first there was a waiting period when his vocation would be tested. He sent him to his cell with the words 'Go to your cell and your cell will teach you everything.' The young man went, full of expectation. Something marvellous would happen and he would know beyond doubt that God wanted him to be a monk. For the first few hours it felt good, but after a while the youth got hungry and a little bit bored, so he went in search of the abbot, who sent him back with the words 'Go to your cell and your cell will teach you everything.' He returned somewhat chastened and tried to pray, but his mind was full of grand plans of what he would do when he was a monk and he could not settle to pray. He went to the abbot again in frustration, and again the abbot sent him back to his cell. This time his mind filled with all kinds of wild things, unpleasant images and fearful imaginings. He ran again to the abbot, who sent him back: 'Go to your cell and your cell will teach you everything.' This went on for days, which turned into weeks and then into months. The youth became resigned to his situation and stayed in his cell, although he was bored and downcast and now entertained few hopes of ever becoming a monk. One day he picked up some pieces of straw from the floor of his cell and began to twist them into threads. Soon he was weaving a basket and found that after some time he had stopped watching the hours go by and had been wholly absorbed in his task. When he next saw the abbot, the wise old senior monk said to him: 'Now you are ready to begin.'

The youth was alone in his cell while he had to endure this hard process of being stripped, but he had a wise and older guide to accompany him and help him locate himself in the process of finding his true path.

Teachers of prayer have long referred to two different traditions, known as kataphatic and apophatic, both of which are discernible in Scripture. Kataphatic prayer is the more familiar and relies on concrete images to aid prayer – creation, candles, icons, ritual and so on. Practitioners of this kind of prayer describe their relationship with God in visual or sensual terms, often using vivid imagery. They find God in the created world of experience and the senses. Apophatic prayer rejects all this, preferring to remain speechless before the mystery and hiddenness of God. It is sometimes called the *via negativa* – the way of not knowing. It is reluctant to use words or try to describe what God is like, and seeks the simplicity of naked being before God. Kataphatic prayer is a bit like praying with our eyes open; apophatic prayer more like with our eyes shut. Both types have come under suspicion from those who hold the Bible in high regard, yet God's word is not unfavourable to either tradition. We find concrete images in Scripture to describe God. God is a mother nurturing her child, a shepherd guiding his sheep and so on. But there is also mystery and an acknowledgement that wonder and silent awe are appropriate as we approach the living God: Moses ascending the mountain into the cloud; Paul caught up into the seventh heaven;

John on the island of Patmos experiencing silence in heaven for 'about half an hour' (Rev. 8.1). God is a speaking God who wants to be known, but we cannot say everything there is to be said. There is mystery, and in recognizing our creatureliness we are called to bow in awe and reverence before our Creator who reaches down to whisper and thunder to us through the vastness of divine love.

The language of prayer

In his reflections on prayer, Eugene Peterson describes three different types of language: the language of intimacy and relationship; of information, which we use to learn about the world; of motivation, which we use to make things happen and persuade. The language he is interested in is that of intimacy, because this is the language of prayer.[5] It is this kind, however, that becomes less fluent in our lives as we grow up. We turn to language for information and facts instead of relating. This is the language that bombards us 24/7 and banishes quiet from our lives. Lovers and new parents recover relational language for a while, and poets and songwriters operate in it, but in the main it languishes in neglect. It is perhaps a pity that English has lost the intimate forms of 'thee' and 'thou' because they evoke the relational so well. In prayer we are seeking to use and develop this relational language once more. Prayer is the language in which we talk to God in trust and intimacy, and so it is through prayer that we practise this relational language.

As we explore the vast terrain that is the life of prayer we learn to put on, to inhabit, the virtues of Christian character (see Rom. 5.3–5; 2 Pet. 1.5–7). We learn patience as we wait on God's time, knowing that 'this also must pass' (Anglo-Saxon proverb) and that our loving heavenly father has prepared for us 'such things as pass our understanding' (Book of Common Prayer, Collect for the 6th Sunday after Trinity). We learn persistence as we ponder the friend at midnight and the widow pestering the unjust judge and meditate on those things we have been bringing before God for years and years. We find out what it means to endure and how endurance produces character, which leads on to hope. Part of this is learning to ask for what we believe God wants to do and what it is in God's character to do, rather than what we think God should do. To cultivate hope is to be set free from the things that contract our view and shrink our faith.

Christian hope, we discover, is everywhere in the Scriptures, always looking forward and always firmly grounded in the person of Christ himself. Such hope does not disappoint us (Rom 5.5). It will expand our vision as we learn to discern its presence in the world around us, signs of God's kingdom growing secretly – small perhaps, but significant and full of new life.

Mystical prayer

Mysticism has had a very bad press among certain schools of Christian thought. It is regarded as highly suspect, something that begins in mist and ends in schism and leads only to a preoccupation with feelings, in particular the desire for ecstatic experiences in prayer.[6] Since only a small minority of Christians ever have such an experience, mysticism is viewed as elitist and highly unusual. But this is to adopt a very narrow and exclusive understanding of what mysticism is really about, and misses the point of the relationship at the heart of prayer. The heart of mysticism is simply union with God, which is the objective reality of every Christian believer. Its origins lie in the New Testament, where the word *mysterion* means 'that which is needing to be revealed'. Thus in Colossians 1.26 Paul writes, 'the mystery that has been hidden throughout the ages and generations but has now been revealed to his saints', and goes on to state, 'the riches of the glory of this mystery, which is Christ in you, the hope of glory' (v. 27). Mysticism is, as Thomas Merton pointed out, following the apostle Paul, the normal way of Christian perfection.[7] Furthermore it lies at the heart of Christian spirituality in that it concerns our union with God accomplished by Jesus Christ through the Holy Spirit. In the Incarnation, death and resurrection of Christ, God has drawn near to us, and as we receive Spirit-filled new life, we are united with the godhead.

God is a mystery, but the most mysterious thing of all where human beings are concerned is that we should be invited into this mystery to share God's life and to experience the Lord in love and communion. Mysticism thus understood, and having its roots in the Trinity and in the New Testament, is open to all. The philosopher of religion Louis Dupré defined mystical as 'all that refers to faith as it directly affects human experience [including] the common Christian intimation of a divine presence in scripture, religious doctrine, liturgy and nature'.[8]

Eli and Samuel

One of the most instructive instances of spiritual direction in the Old Testament is the story of Eli and his young charge Samuel in 1 Samuel 3.1–18. The word of the Lord was rare at that time and even in the courts of the temple the divine presence was not obvious. The story is a reminder that God's voice can come unexpectedly, when we are least ready. How many people go on a retreat expecting God to speak to them, only to hear the Spirit's voice while washing up a few days later? Samuel was in bed when he heard his name called. Three times he responded by going to Eli and announcing 'Here I am, for you called me.' Each time Eli sent him back until on the third occasion he realized that it must be God calling. Eli knew enough of God's ways to get there eventually and was able to get out of the way so that Samuel could respond. Eli was slow in grasping what was happening, but now at last both he and Samuel were listening with their antennae tuned to the right wavelength. He told Samuel that if it happened again he should say 'Speak, Lord, for your servant is listening' (v. 9). In fact Eli was not important. As in all instances of spiritual direction, there are three persons involved, and the Holy Spirit was present and active here. Eli mediated but it was God speaking to Samuel that mattered. It was enough that Eli could put Samuel before his own needs. All directors have to learn that, having fulfilled their role, they have to step off the stage. Eli is also a reminder that we can be used by God even in the midst of our own brokenness. Whether we are avid seekers or blissfully unaware that God might be calling to us, this story teaches clearly that it is always God who takes the initiative. In Samuel's case, even though he was learning to commit his whole life to serving in the Lord's temple, he did not know that God had something personal to say to him. We recall at this point that Jesus did not always find the synagogue the easiest place to reach people. He taught as he walked; he spoke on the mountain and the plain, in people's homes and on the seashore. He uses the ordinary and everyday to speak to us but, like Samuel, we may need a helping hand to learn how to listen.

Jesus and prayer

It goes without saying that Jesus himself, the living Word, is the model director in Scripture. We are given glimpses of Jesus' prayer life in the Gospels in ways that can help us in our own, and from reflecting on Jesus' life we also learn much about practising the presence of God in all our daily encounters. He taught his disciples about prayer and put into practice the things he said about spending time with his heavenly father. If we are seeking intimacy with the creator of the universe, Jesus is a good starting place for us.

Spiritual direction focuses particularly on the Holy Spirit as the real director, and in the life of Jesus we witness a Spirit-filled life enabling him to live according to the will of God. Again he had important things to say to his disciples about the Spirit and his work that we will need to heed and discover for ourselves. The resources we need for living – wisdom, strength, insight and power of the right kind – come from the Holy Spirit within us, enabling us to live for God at each moment.

Meditating on the life of Jesus will be perhaps the most constant reminder that giving time to developing our relationship with God is not for ourselves only. While he knew deep intimacy with God the father, Jesus lived his life facing outwards towards the world, available to go where God sent him, exercising compassion on everyone he met. We cannot follow Jesus and live exclusive self-centred lives. This is an area where spiritual direction needs constant awareness.

Particularly relevant for the subject of this book is the way we see Jesus himself turning to Scripture in the Gospels. We see him reading from it in his faith community; he referred to it constantly in his teaching and his encounters with others, especially the religious leaders of his time. We see him unfolding the Scriptures to his disciples and explaining them. We even see him challenging Satan on how not to use the Bible. To his disciples he emphasized the importance of hearing his word and doing it, and we cannot separate this command from the purpose of spiritual direction. Although Jesus quoted the Hebrew Bible to the devil and to the religious leaders, his approach to the many people he met was in essence relational. He paused for them, touched them, listened to them, looked at them, made a request, asked a question, told a story. He listened to God and he understood people, and in the Gospels we have a range of examples of him in the role of director.

Jesus, the master spiritual director

A single passage, Mark 6, provides an example with many lessons for anyone who is a spiritual director. The disciples in this chapter come to Jesus to tell him about their activities and he invites them to come apart to a place of solitude with him. People come to us with their doings and concerns and need to be given a quiet space where they can talk at length, probably in no particular order of events but freely enabling a narrative to emerge out of which the Holy Spirit may be discerned.

A meeting with a spiritual director can be like pressing the pause button, stopping to draw breath and finding refreshment for the continuance of the journey. The gift of hospitable space enables this to happen in a fruitful and unthreatening way. It is often at the resting place that the Holy Spirit can finally get a word in edgeways as the stuff of life is sifted. No wonder that the disciples were irritated by the crowd who muscled in and stole their precious time apart with Jesus (vv. 35–36). These others were a distraction and were invading their space, spoiling their communion with the Lord. This happens over and over again in life, but perhaps these are the very moments in which God wants to show us more of God's self. Here Jesus turns the apparent distraction into the material for direction and gives the disciples a challenge: 'You give them something to eat' (v. 37). He wants the disciples to learn from the distraction and to learn by doing. Afterwards Jesus left them and went away to spend time alone with God, which was important following an intense time of active ministry. He was not the kind of spiritual director who was available 24/7 and apt to suffer rapid burnout because of it. His communion with his heavenly father in prayer was his absolute priority. The result was that when he returned to his disciples he was in total command of the situation, which in every other way looked out of control. There are times when a director needs to reject the non-directive stance – so beloved of counsellors – and take charge. Knowing what to do, when, will only come as we learn to pay attention through prayer to what God is doing in us and bowing at all times to God's authority in us. Jesus got into the boat, calmed the raging storm and urged the disciples not to be afraid (v. 50). By staying with the storms that hit our directees, by remaining calm ourselves and by reminding them that God repeatedly tells us in Scripture not to be afraid, we encourage those in turmoil to know that they are held in God's grip, no matter what happens. Directive though he is, Jesus' words to his disciples are gentle and comforting. He does not show up their ignorance by drawing attention to the loaves and fishes Mark says they did not understand. He does not hector them or reproach them. In this sense we are always to be non-judgemental, mindful of the fact that it is the Holy Spirit's job to convict, not ours. Jesus goes at their pace, is patient with their fumbling hearts and minds, waits to lead them further on when they are ready. Sometimes our directees will sound like stuck records, playing the same passage over and over again. To force them on, tell them to get over it – whatever 'it' is – or suggest by our body language that we are bored or irritated by their slowness may close down the conversation and lose the opportunity to hear at last what God has to say about the situation. There may be no other place except the person's own head to work out what is really going on. Throughout Mark's Gospel Jesus is prepared to comfort but also confront, always knowing which approach to take with whoever is before him. There is no sense that the Christian way is a series of hoops through which we have to jump at predetermined times in order to grow. Again and again Jesus stayed with people and their situations, encouraging them to reflect on what was happening and refusing to allow them to deflect the conversation to other things, especially what other people were saying or doing.

The woman of Samaria

The classic example of avoidance on the part of the directee and Jesus' determination to address the real issue was his encounter with the woman of Samaria in John 4. Tired though he was by his travels, Jesus was able to set aside his own needs in order to meet this woman in all hers. Although we normally expect the director to provide hospitality, here Jesus asks the woman for a drink. By doing so he began with something to which she could relate. Asking for a drink afforded her some dignity and enabled her to do something for him. He spoke readily of spiritual things and was direct in his approach with the woman. Although directors are in a listening role, this time is for the specific purpose of talking about God and often it is the opening question that is key, unlocking the door to the sacred things hidden in the human heart. Beginning with a basic human need for a drink of water, an ordinary part of life, Jesus turned it around into a deep spiritual question. Gently but persistently he enabled the woman to open her spiritual eyes and grow in spiritual awareness. Jesus spoke to the woman with restraint but spoke nevertheless. He told her what she needed to hear when she could bear it. The woman wanted to wriggle off the hook and turn the conversation to something more comfortable and much less personal, but Jesus was not to be deflected. He persisted with what might have seemed a disastrous policy of revealing the woman's dubious situation, but ultimately his words brought life, healing and hope to her. The ministry of spiritual direction is about the good news of the gospel, though there may be times when directors feel they are the bearers of bad news. In this story the conversation was centred on who Jesus was. It is a central issue for every Christian at every stage of life: Who is Jesus for me today? Is he Lord today? Is he accommodating my questions or challenging me to trust and honour him in spite of them? Is he my saviour even in this desperate situation? Is he wanting to show me more of himself as my brother, my friend, my lover, my Lord?

The conversation continued because Jesus made the woman feel safe enough to reveal things about herself. He was not shocked or condemning in his response to her, which made possible an encounter that changed her. She felt known and loved: 'Come and see a man who told me everything I have ever done!' (v. 29). She honestly witnessed to her new-found awareness, so that even at this stage the Holy Spirit could work through as well as in her, bringing others to meet Jesus for themselves. To know we are loved for who we are and in spite of ourselves is a gift beyond compare. To be known by God and loved by our loving Lord is the good news that God wants everyone to hear.

At the end of this story it is worth noting that the woman went back home, which must have been hard to do. She was not the only one to be sent home by Jesus, back into difficult situations, vulnerable and alone. The people who unburden themselves and reveal secrets to their directors also have in the main to go back whence they came, where difficult issues remain. We cannot go with them and we cannot rescue them. The same Holy Spirit who has been the focus of the hour of spiritual conversation goes with them, however, and having gained awareness of God's ways in the middle of their struggles, they can be reassured that the Lord will continue to be there working in them and through them. There are many people like this Samaritan woman who live life on the margins of society and fear that the Church will reinforce their sense of unworthiness. Finding someone who is willing to listen may be the first step towards the realization that in God's eyes they too are sons and daughters of Abraham and are invited to share God's hospitality.

In his meeting with the woman we see Jesus applying a working knowledge of his tradition and his awareness of the concerns of outsiders towards religious questions. He was steeped in the Scriptures and drew on them in the most incisive yet natural way to get to the heart of the matter. His use of the Old Testament was both orthodox and authoritative as well as refreshing; and it offered an invitation to see it in new and often startling ways that cut to the core of the issue. This dual approach is worth studying for all its worth to reach a humble kind of ease and confidence in applying Scripture to each and every situation before us. The Bible may be a poultice to a wounded soul, the balm of Gilead itself. It may also be a sword, cutting to the quick, or the surgeon's knife required to lance the boil that is poisoning the lifeblood of a needy individual. Again, it is important to let the Holy Spirit decide what is needed as we listen with the person for the hand of God in the story.

Bartimaeus

In Mark 10.46–52 Jesus met blind Bartimaeus, a man who was an embarrassment to his friends and who had to overcome certain obstacles to get to Jesus. Here was another outcast searching for hope and who discovered the living Word, Jesus Christ, through a personal encounter. Bartimaeus' friends tried to hold him back and in the end he took things into his own hands and threw off his cloak – possibly the only thing he owned – to make what was for him the long journey to meet the Lord. Although spiritual direction brings to light people desperately trying to avoid truly hearing God, there are many others equally desperate to know the Lord's healing touch and hear the living Word speaking to them. Bartimaeus was one of the latter. Mark wrote that Jesus 'stood still' (v. 49). He stopped and gave Bartimaeus his attention. Attentiveness is the one gift directors can give to those who come to talk to them. We do not know how long Jesus stood still while Bartimaeus made his way over to him, but we know he asked Bartimaeus: 'What do you want me to do for you?' (v. 51). Again, he afforded Bartimaeus true dignity by not assuming, not imposing, not crushing his identity. Bartimaeus had to do the work. It can be tempting as directors to make assumptions and think we know what those before us need, to do the work for them. Bartimaeus, in the story as Mark tells it, knew instantly what he wanted: he wanted to see. For many people seeking spiritual growth it may take much longer to know what it is they truly want.

It is also worth pondering where Bartimaeus' request would lead him. We rejoice in the restoration of his sight – of course we do. But life for him would never be the same and it would not be all celebration. His old way of begging and relying on others to take him to his favourite spot at the roadside and then home again at night was over for ever. Bartimaeus now had new responsibilities. When light dawns towards new understanding we also face new responsibilities. We cannot remain indifferent once we have eyes to see. This encounter between Jesus and Bartimaeus is a forceful reminder that spiritual direction will lead us back into the world as changed men and women who have heard God's invitation to live differently.

The road to Emmaus

The Gospel account of the encounter of the bereaved disciples walking towards Emmaus with the risen Lord Jesus is perhaps the clearest example of the centrality of the Scriptures to the way God makes God's self known (Luke 24.13–35). Sad and downhearted, Cleopas and his companion had lost all hope that Jesus was the promised Messiah and were trying to make sense of it as they walked along the road. They could not do so by themselves. Spiritual direction is a talking ministry in which we try to make sense of our experience and our glimpses of God's hand in our lives; and as we do, even though we are speaking to another human being, Jesus himself draws near and walks alongside us, desiring to teach us about himself (vv. 15ff.). Notice how Jesus drew alongside the disciples. If we are going to help people draw near to God we have to take them seriously where they are. Jesus' first question to the downcast disciples was a simple one: 'What are you discussing with each other while you walk along?' (Luke 24.17).

The disciples gave a reasonably coherent account of events but it may be that spiritual directors have to help tease out what is important as they listen to half-formed sentences and a jumbled outpouring of words. We see here that Jesus did not harangue them for their lack of insight or faith but simply asked an opening question that enabled them to explain their thoughts and feelings. As they told him all that had happened, Jesus listened for some time before taking them to the Scriptures, walking alongside them as their companion. At this point he confronted them with their lack of faith – a reminder that spiritual directors need to be able to ask tough questions as well as open-ended ones, and sometimes say things that are hard to hear. He began at the beginning and 'interpreted to them the things about himself in all the scriptures' (v. 27). For today's seekers there may be very little context in which to interpret their spiritual experience. We may need to drip-feed them the word of God, but if they are hungry to know it is often the case that they will devour any opportunity to learn. One of the first things to inspire me to read the Bible for myself was the story of Mary Jones and her Bible. Mary was a young Welsh girl who could not read or write, but on learning about Jesus' love for her, walked many miles to obtain a copy of the Bible. Such stories of individuals who cannot read taking up Bible study in earnest and drinking in the background to the Scriptures, so that they can understand, continue the world over (see Chapter 9 for using the Bible with non-literate people).

Jesus opened the eyes of the disciples on the road to Emmaus so that they could see him afresh through the eyes of the Scriptures. The story does not end here for he continued with them, and when they invited him to stay, he did so. As with the woman of Samaria, discussed above, Jesus was willing to receive as well as give hospitality. As their guest at supper he used a gesture to reconnect them with the Last Supper he had shared with his disciples the night before he died, and by doing so showed them who he was. Thus Scripture and experience unite in the person of Jesus. The disciples were then left to reflect on what had happened and choose what to do about it. They had listened but it was the felt experience of their hearts burning within them that enabled their minds to catch up and understand the significance of what they had heard.

The story of the Road to Emmaus shows us how Jesus uses the whole of Scripture to help us understand him. The disciples were trying to understand the death of Jesus. This story shows the centrality of the mystery of the cross to our lives. It is also the key to understanding the Scriptures.

It shows how the Lord is willing to work with our feelings. The disciples were sad and perplexed. They expressed how hope had been dashed. We need to bring all these feelings into prayer. Articulating them in spiritual direction enables them to be brought to the surface so that the Holy Spirit can work in us.

Finally, the invitation to stay and eat with them shows the disciples' desire to be in Jesus' presence. We need to invite Jesus in, to stay with him in prayer so that we can respond to his self-revelation.

More encounters

There are many other examples of Jesus doing the work of spiritual direction in the Gospels. In Luke 10 he was tested by a lawyer who wanted to catch him out. Spiritual directors will be tested for all kinds of reasons. Sometimes directees will be looking for truth and authenticity and wondering whether they are looking in the right place as they sit with their director. Sometimes they will be resisting the Holy Spirit and projecting their resistance on to the director because they cannot openly defy God or are perhaps not even aware they are refusing to respond to the divine call. It is interesting to note that Jesus responded to the lawyer by telling him a story.

In Luke 19 Jesus took the initiative with a man who was playing hide and seek with him and invited himself to his house. Zacchaeus was hiding in a tree because he wanted to see Jesus, and his secret desire led to a face-to-face meeting that changed his life. As the story has been handed down to us, Zacchaeus began with a compromise, which Jesus accepted. Each person is different and God knows how much reality we can bear at any one time. We do not know whether Zacchaeus went any further or whether he became a regular disciple. Jesus, it appears, leaves us to decide. This is brought out even more clearly in the story of the rich man in Mark 10.17–22. Here was a zealous man who wanted to do the right thing and something inside him told him Jesus could help him. He came seeking and Jesus gave him his time and attention. Like many people in direction he was eager to say what had gone right and rehearsed his ability to keep the commandments. Jesus looked at him with love and went straight to the point by putting his finger on the one thing preventing him from following. His attachment to wealth was the spiritual blockage that held him in its grip. Attachments can be anything that we hold on to in such a way that they keep us from becoming the people God wants us to be. Hence St Ignatius' fierce-sounding insistence that we 'rid' ourselves of anything that hinders us and 'make ourselves indifferent to all created things'.[9] The man went away shocked and grieving and Jesus did not go after him. Who knows whether or not he wrestled with his attachment until he could let it go, but it is unlikely that God had anything else to say to him until he did. There are times when the spiritual director has to let people walk away, not knowing whether or not they will come back. Jesus was not flattered by the man's praise of him (v. 17) or manipulated into chasing him when things did not go his way. He simply spoke the truth with love and compassion.

There are many other examples of spiritual direction discernible in the Bible. Eli and Hannah, Ruth and Naomi, Jethro and Moses, Paul and Timothy, Samuel and David, Job and his three friends. Some, like the last example, show us how not to do it – though the friends did at least sit in silence with their stricken friend at the beginning.

Prayer and personality

'Pray as you can, not as you can't' has become something of a cliché in writings about prayer, but it is a vitally important lesson to learn. Many people have never been taught to pray or, if they have, it has rarely extended beyond the basics. We expect prayer to be difficult and devour books on the subject, but often we find ourselves struggling uphill overloaded with baggage. Believing that God is reaching out to us long before we turn to prayer is perhaps the first thing we need to grasp. Learning to pray with the grain is not far behind. People interested in retreats and finding help in prayer will soon come across various workshops on personality, especially the Myers-Briggs Type Indicator (MBTI). Where MBTI workshops focus on prayer and personality, they can open up a whole new range of possibilities that set us free from the sense that we are hopeless at prayer. They can also feed us in ways that suit our temperaments. As Paul said in Romans 12.4–5: 'For as in one body we have many members, and not all the members have the same function, so we, who are many, are one body in Christ, and individually we are members one of another.' He also made the important point that 'We have gifts that differ according to the grace given to us' (Rom. 12.6).

It is indeed true that 'Who we are is how we pray.' Spiritual directors of course need to have this at the front of their minds at all times so that they do not impose their own way of praying on someone else. There are good books available that explain what the MBTI is all about,[10] and some offer examples of prayer and reading the Scriptures for different personality types.[11] Some of the ways of using Scripture in spiritual direction described in this book will suit some people more than others. At a very basic level some of us are drawn to more meditative practices of reading, and enjoy the silence and stillness necessary to settle into prayer. Others are eager to hear the word and do it. They are likely to be more extrovert in personality and have a preference for action over contemplation. Spiritual directors need to be able to work with both types, and may find it important to remind the person in front of them that the Church needs both. For if the Church abandons the habit of setting aside time to seek God in prayer it will forever waste its energy in programmes and activities that it is not clear God has initiated; while if it withdraws into prayer to the exclusion of action it will quickly become disconnected from the rest of the world and unable to proclaim the good news either in word or deed.

Growth in self-acceptance and in acceptance of others comes as we accept who we are and do not wish everyone else was like us. Rather we rejoice in our gifts, which differ yet complement each other. Where Scripture is concerned there will be some who like a systematic way of reading through the Bible, paying attention to detail, perhaps enjoying getting to know the original languages and picking up the nuances of the text in the Hebrew and Greek. They may stay with a single verse and happily return to it again and again. Others like the bigger picture and dive in wherever it feels right. They are more likely to revel in new ways of reading, which might include allowing a longer passage to enfold them in its narrative. Some people are thinkers and want to study with the help of commentaries and dictionaries, while others prefer imagining what it must have felt like to be one of the individuals who met Jesus and shared a meal or walked along the road with him. The point is that all these ways are valid, and it is useful to know ourselves better so that we know what works best for us. This will help us remain open to trying new ways that stretch us and open our eyes to further dimensions of how God speaks to us.

Certain Bible passages will appeal to different personality types too. Some love John's Gospel because of its rich symbolism and mystery – they recognize the way glory is revealed in a suffering saviour. Others love the way Jesus often responded to a question with one of his own. Thinking types often like Matthew's Gospel because of its ordered structure, while feeling types turn to the story of the road to Emmaus and the response of the disciples after supper: 'Were not our hearts burning within us . . .?' (Luke 24.32).

9

Spiritual direction and non-literate approaches to Scripture

For someone like me the most natural way of reflecting on the Scriptures is to read them and books about them. As an English woman born in the twentieth century who went through the education system and now teaches theology, that is my world. But as someone who has also been a mother of a young child, a daughter of frail and elderly parents whose eyes were dim and also a part-time prison chaplain, I have been made aware that books and reading are not for everyone. I am also a historian by training and have both explored the world prior to the printing press and learned to live in the digital age. We are so used to the ubiquity of the printed word on paper and screen that we are apt to forget that for centuries there was no printed word, and even now there are many people who cannot read or for whom books are an alien realm.

We have been considering a word-based ministry built on conversation. Using the Bible is about using words. We are seeking to know a God who has spoken, who communicates. There are times for all of us, however, when words run dry or feel inadequate or even intrusive. How do we remain faithful to the word when we cannot find any of our own? The aim here is to explore ways we can engage with the text that do not involve reading. Another motive behind this chapter is the common perception that spiritual direction is only for educated middle-class people. Its association with the retreat movement – retreats are expensive and impossible for many – has reinforced this image. But spiritual direction is possible for anyone – and it is not only about reading.

The place of listening

I have been struck while writing this book with the emphasis there is to be placed on listening over reading. In my own experience I have found that hearing the word of God read or recited aloud has had a far greater impact than reading it myself in silence. Learning and speaking it aloud myself has had even greater influence on my ability to hear the words afresh, and the same is true when sharing words from Scripture with a soul friend or spiritual director. Why is this? When we read, it is usually with a predetermined purpose. We have our own agenda, whether we are seeking information, in which case we read quickly to get to the gist of the meaning, or we read for instruction to be able to achieve something. Even reading for pleasure is done so that we can relax, so if it does not achieve that we move on to something else. Allowing God to set the agenda is to read differently, and hearing someone else read to us helps us to allow the word to take charge. The text can now do something to and for us. Ideally the reader will read slowly, so that our minds can slow down also – and if we are listening in the context of worship, we have already begun to open up to the Holy Spirit's presence. In *Reading with God*, David Foster muses that listening is perhaps more important than understanding, and notes that although the disciples often failed to understand what Jesus was saying, they did not stop listening to him.[1] When my son was small I sometimes wanted to intervene in conversations between him and his father because the latter made few concessions to his son's age when it came to vocabulary. I heard him explaining engines and how they worked in great detail, our son hanging on every word. He could not have grasped more than the mere gist of what he heard, but kept coming back for more because he was gripped with fascination for these strange objects and wanted to know about them. I wonder if it was also because he loved the sound of the words too, the rhythm and texture of them and the way he was addressed directly rather than spoken down to. Slowly but surely he came to understand the meaning of the words and concepts. As a result he has come to be familiar with the world of the engine and shows no signs of boredom or having outgrown it.

Entering strange new worlds

For people like me who were brought up with it, the King James Version of the Bible may sound familiar. The language is strange but the sound of the words and the richness of their imagery draw us in and we can dwell in them even when we do not yet entirely understand their meaning. Gradually the sense becomes clearer and, as with poetry, it yields fresh meaning as time goes on. There is much to ponder here, given that the Scriptures, like poetry, were originally designed to be listened to rather than read. Even though the Jews are people of the book and Christians have always valued literacy because of the place of sacred literature in their faith, both have given an important place to the public hearing of Scripture. In synagogues and in the early Christian fellowships they gathered together to hear God's word. We have examples of this in the Bible itself. In the Old Testament, Ezra the scribe read aloud to the people from the book of the Law following the return from exile in Babylon (Neh. 8.1–12). The people's response is also recorded, for they paid close attention to the reading, which was interpreted for them so they could understand (v. 8). There was weeping (v. 9), rejoicing and worship as a result (v. 12). The letters of the apostle Paul were not copied and passed around individuals but read aloud when everyone gathered to worship. Even his letters to individuals like Timothy and Titus were soon counted among the sacred literature Christians held authoritative and heard read in their assemblies. With the onset of monasticism, meditative listening to Scripture read aloud became a major component of life for monks and nuns. In churches, chapels, cathedrals and homes, people still listen today. The advent of smartphones, tablets and so on means that many more people can enter this listening world, though the big difference is that listening through headphones is a solitary occupation. Hearing God's word spoken aloud offers opportunities for dramatic readings, recitations, acted-out readings and so on. Once sitting in church my heart sank when it was announced that we were going to listen to the whole of Psalm 119 read aloud. In fact there were two readers, who had practised hard, and the result was electrifying as the entire psalm came alive and leapt off the page. At other times I have learned the passage of Scripture that I have planned to preach from and declaimed rather than read it. How different the word of God sounds and how powerful when it is spoken instead of read. Directors might encourage their directees to learn some verses of Scripture – perhaps a Psalm that means a lot to them – so that they can carry God's living Word with them in their hearts rather than in their pockets in a book.

Poetry and painters

One of the striking features of poetry is that it tells us what we already know but in words we could not have found for ourselves. Some people who are wordsmiths can express their thoughts in poetry better than prose. Spiritual directors who have encouraged their directees to try expressing their thoughts and emotions in poetry may well be the catalyst that unlocks a poetic gift. In the seventh century St Hilda encouraged the cowherd Caedmon, who thought he had nothing to offer the community at Whitby, to write verse, and Caedmon went on to turn many of the great Christian themes into poetry and song for the blessing of others.[2]

I have often been given a poem by my spiritual director, and when my own words have run out these carefully crafted lines have helped me to express what I want to say to God. Poetry as a genre, of course, has a thoroughly biblical foundation since so much of the Bible is itself in poetic form. Prophets, Psalms, indeed all the Wisdom literature, are poetry. Eugene Peterson has reflected on how easy it is to abuse words, and that spiritual leaders in particular are prone to flatter, manipulate and subtly exercise power via the words they choose. Spiritual directors may also be placed in this category. Poetry invites us to reverence the words we use. 'Poets are caretakers of language, the shepherds of words, keeping them from harm, exploitation, misuse.'[3] Both Scripture and poetry have the power to enable us to hear ourselves better as we recognize ourselves through carefully crafted words. In our role as spiritual directors, Peterson's words are a timely check to reflect on how we use words with those in our care. Using the Scriptures in the direction setting means that at all times we are to be aware of the power of words and so maintain respect and reverence for them. There is an artistry in the text of the Bible that means it often aims to show us rather than instruct. Jesus' parables are the obvious example of this. Good art does not give closure but invites those who see to probe and thus see further, thereby being drawn into a new and different mode of reality. We see glimpses and traces of the divine hand in the Scriptures that draw us in.

The great artists have helped us to understand our culture better. They have drawn, painted and sculpted the essence of what it means to be human in a given time and place, and we need to pay attention to them in order to understand ourselves. Prior to the printing press, art also taught people the faith, and from stained glass windows for the common people to expensive commissions by the wealthy, Christian themes dominated for centuries. Most artists who have a Christian faith prefer to describe themselves as Christians who do art rather than Christian artists or people who do Christian art, and they are an important reminder for the rest of us that all of life is lived under God and that there are not Christian and non-Christian bits. Such dualism lies latent in the thinking of many Christians and is often revealed through spiritual direction. God is interested in the whole of us, not only when we have on our 'Sunday best' or are doing something overtly 'religious'.

Creative prayer

One of the ways we can seek to return to a more integrated way of living is through exploring different types of praying. Many churches experiment imaginatively in this area. Some prayer activities continue to be word-based – writing names on a card and hanging it on a prayer tree, writing a letter to God and so on. Others are more visual. Can prayer be visual? In Scripture we discover that the heavens are telling the glory of God, but there are no words (Ps. 19.1–4).

What about when there is a language barrier? When words fail us and we struggle to express the depths of emotion we feel? When tears seem the only form of prayer we can offer? There are times when words are simply not adequate. Indeed the Incarnation should alert us to this fact, for the word became flesh and made his home among us, thus making the word tangible in the person of Jesus. In his letter to the Romans, Paul states that when words fail us in prayer the Holy Spirit intercedes for us 'with sighs too deep for words' (Rom. 8.26). The Bible goes further still in indicating that prayer involves the whole of our being, our bodies as well as our minds and lips. Moses lifted his hands in prayer as the Israelites fought in battle (Exod. 17.8–16); Miriam led the people in a celebratory dance following the crossing of the Red Sea (Exod. 15.20; cf. 2 Sam. 6.14); the psalmists urge us to bow down to God in worship and to lift our hands in praise (Pss. 5.7; 134.2); John the apostle fell down in awe when God spoke to him (Rev. 1.17) and Jesus knelt in agony as he prayed in Gethsemane (Luke 22.41). One of the ways a director can help with prayer is to encourage directees to think about the physical aspects of praying, such as where to pray and what posture to adopt. Simple breathing exercises can help us slow down and focus in a way that engages our whole person. This can help with distractions and the ability to stay present. Directors might then go on to suggest using the body more in prayer, through gesture, dance or other movement. How might prayers of contrition, for example, be changed by beating one's breast?

Many have put their prayers into music, painting and dance and discovered they do not have to be great artists to do so. There are a number of spiritual directors who have found great possibilities in using artistic forms of communication. Some are also trained in art therapy and use this as part of their ministry. Even without such skills, an experienced director knows that speaking may not always be the best way to convey what God is doing in someone's life and is able to encourage directees to express their relationship with God in non-verbal ways. Love, joy, peace, forgiveness, support can all be shown in non-verbal ways, and Scripture more than hints at some of the possibilities. The real point of spiritual direction concerns what we do when we leave the session, so such practical demonstrations of what God is saying to us are vital.

If there is anxiety about whether all this is prayer, reassurance is found in the Scriptures. The sons of Asaph, Heman and Jeduthun prophesied with lyres, harps and cymbals (1 Chron. 25.1). Bezalel was given direct artistic gifts by God 'to devise artistic designs, to work in gold, silver, and bronze, in cutting stones for setting, and in carving wood, in every kind of craft' (Exod. 31.1–5). His artistic gifts were to be directed towards the beautification of the tent of meeting, where the Ark of the Covenant resided – in other words, the place where God met with the people and communicated with them. Here is prayer in action, expressed through the visual as well as the rituals of worship.

There are occasions when visual prayer becomes a necessity. There may be a language barrier, for example. How may we express what is on our hearts so that the others praying with us can join in our prayer? At a prayer meeting it may be enough for each to pray in their own language, but there are other occasions when words will not suffice, and in the often deep moments of spiritual direction, something other needs to enable expression. Someone in agony that runs too deep for words may need to draw, paint or move their body in a silent cry to God. Someone else may sing or dance for joy.

I am married to a sculptor and we have experimented with retreats using pieces of sculpture to invite participants to observe, touch and reflect with them. Having been given ample time to look, people are then invited to say what came to mind. This is not meant to entail sophisticated theology, and many would be surprised to hear that they are reflecting theologically through what they say, but the purpose is to speak from the heart about whatever the image before them has evoked. They are then invited to think of a verse or passage of Scripture that is invoked by their reflections and to meditate on that. The sculptor then talks about what was in his mind as he sculpted, and finally people are invited to make responses of their own. This may be a prayer or poem, or perhaps something more concrete, using found materials that express what they wish to say to God of what has arisen out of the day. Sculpture, prayer and Scripture thus inform each other and help people make connections that are relevant to their lives and encourage their horizons to expand, their faith to grow.[4]

For the Eastern Orthodox Church the visual has played an essential role for faith through icons. Icons were essential in a world where people could not read. More recently they have become familiar in the West and are valued by many Christians of all traditions. Icons are intended to be a window through which we pass in order to encounter God. They often depict Bible characters such as Moses and Elijah, and invite us to reflect on their experience of God. They have particular rules of composition and symbolic meanings and each one is prayed as the artist 'writes' it. Icons have a different kind of relevance in a world where we are saturated with words to the extent that they often mean very little. Ann Persson has written a captivating account of how one famous icon, Rublev's *Icon of the Trinity*, nourished her faith during a time of serious illness. Strapped to a stretcher face down for two weeks due to a back injury, she asked for a copy of the icon and began to gaze and meditate on it. Slowly it drew her in and she experienced the presence of God in a powerful and deeply felt way.[5]

The Eucharist

Of course the most visual act of worship in the Church is the Eucharist, where word and sacrament meet and become tangible in bread and wine. Eating and drinking involve taste, touch, sight and smell, and as we listen to the word accompanying the gestures, so all our senses are engaged. There have been times in its history when spiritual direction has been closely associated with confession, and the natural conclusion to confessing our sins is to join a worshipping congregation and come to the foot of the cross in Holy Communion. This is what Christians have done since the beginning – reading is not required in order to participate.

10

Alone and together in spiritual direction

Communities are fundamental to the Church

When we turn to the New Testament and read the Gospels we discover that discipleship is something learned on the hoof in company with other disciples. Jesus taught his disciples by first of all calling them to be with him: 'Come and follow me' was his initial invitation. In John 1, two of John the Baptist's disciples asked Jesus where he lived. 'Come and see' was his invitation to them. They listened to his teaching and watched him healing the sick. Then he sent them out in pairs to do the same. Discipleship was a kind of apprenticeship undertaken alongside others. This basic pattern has been repeated over and over again in Christian history. The monasteries, St Francis and his companions, the Beguines in the Low Countries, John Wesley and the early Methodists all understood the importance of the relationship between fellowship and spiritual growth.

Bishop Kallistos Ware regards spiritual direction as originally something done in groups. The major schools of spiritual direction have all expected that direction takes place in a communal setting. Among the desert fathers and mothers the abbas and ammas collected small groups of disciples around them who imitated their way of life and prayer. We tend to think of them as solitary and indeed some were, but even the most curmudgeonly recognized, as St Antony put it: 'Our life and death is with our neighbour.'[1] The life of prayer made these men and women more, not less sensitive to one another.

The Rule of St Benedict, written for a monastic setting, naturally takes for granted the communal aspect, but it is worth considering the implications of this for direction. It is understood that we cannot separate spiritual guidance from the totality of living and so we look in vain for specific rules about spiritual direction in the *Rule*. Even today, Benedictines tend to be cautious about offering spiritual direction except to their own brothers and sisters because it is part of the formation of a person into the Benedictine way of life. The practice of *lectio* that the Benedictines have fostered lends itself especially to communal listening to Scripture, and it is my experience that such times of deep listening together have yielded profound insight that I would not have gleaned alone. Reading slowly and prayerfully, leaving plenty of quiet space and simply receiving the words of others in the room concerning the text, without criticism or comment, is a humbling experience. Kathleen Norris describes her experience of communal *lectio* in a Benedictine monastery in similar terms, pointing out that some had specialist knowledge of Hebrew and Greek and were theologically trained while others had no such qualifications but years of devotional reading behind them.[2] Such diversity would be typical of any monastic community or church congregation. *Lectio divina* is open to all.

At its roots the Anglican tradition is also a communal one. Built on the Book of Common Prayer, the communal element is explicit in the word 'common', meaning commonality and everyday. Traditionally, until relatively recently there has been a worry about elitism in offering direction on a one-to-one basis. One of the traditional strengths of the parish church has been the way everyone is equal as they kneel to pray or stretch out empty hands to receive bread and wine. Rich and poor, old and young, celebrities and unknown citizens together used the same liturgy, and over years of reciting it communally knew many words and phrases from Scripture by heart. They may not have known the term spiritual director, but in many congregations the kind of spiritual direction described by Gordon Jeff, whereby people have sought out those in their congregations who both take prayer seriously and are good listeners, has gone on both on a one-to-one basis and frequently in Lent groups, prayer meetings and home groups.[3]

The Bible is a communal book

The Bible is the Church's book. Public reading of Scripture is part of what Christians do when they meet together, and this important action has formational consequences, just as does personal reading. Reading the Bible draws us into God's wider purposes so that we find our place there. We listen to the difficult as well as the comforting bits and we work together at understanding it. Hearing Scripture read in church is to hear it in the context of sacred time, the Church's calendar, which gives it a particular context and helps us enter a different rhythm. It is also to realize that different parts of the Bible speak differently to people depending on where they are in their lives and circumstances. We all hear the same passage but the person deep in grief will not hear it in the same way as the one who has just fallen in love. Old will hear it one way and young another. All are important. So when we go to see our spiritual director and there are just the two of us in the room, we will recall that this piece of Scripture may be saying something else to our neighbour and may say something new to us in times to come also. Hearing Scripture in church will connect us to the world because its exposition and the church's intercession will help us to go on making new connections, and if the context is also Holy Communion we are reminded that we are being fed so as to serve the Lord when we leave and take up our daily lives once again. The word of God to me is personal but never private.

Eugene Peterson writes of recontextualizing our reading of Scripture into a huge holy community of others who are also reading it. Generation after generation of believers have read and lived the Scriptures, and all over the world continue to do so today. We are part of this great cloud of witnesses.[4]

One of the reasons why spiritual direction needs to stay connected to the Christian Church is that it is a ministry that goes hand in hand with other formational processes going on in the Christian life – it does not stand alone. This should be of great comfort to spiritual directors. Those with whom I have spoken are only too well aware of the enormous responsibility their ministry carries. If wisdom is one of the qualities desirable in a director, the communal aspect of faith becomes all the more essential. The getting of wisdom in Scripture is regarded as a corporate enterprise, and no one is autonomous. In the Old Testament, parents were enjoined to teach their children wisdom, while in the New Testament, the office of teacher was for the benefit of the whole body (see Deut. 6.4–9; Eph. 4.11–12).

Fostering communal reading of Scripture

The Renovaré discipleship programme acknowledges the variety of ways Christian discipleship is fostered in the structure of its formational content, which is designed to be undertaken in groups. Ideally half a dozen people commit to holding one another accountable, and through Scripture, prayer and regular meetings to listen to one another, seek to encourage growth in every area of life. As with all the examples of group direction mentioned here, the importance of trust is central as people share deeply personal things about themselves and their walk with God.[5]

The Northumbria Community is a dispersed community, held together in prayer. Their watchword is 'Alone and together', in recognition that both these aspects of the Christian pilgrimage are important.[6] We may find that each one becomes more relevant at different times in our lives and that like travellers, sometimes we have companions with whom to share the journey and sometimes we have to walk alone. Being transformed into the likeness of Christ means that we engage more fully with the world around us in transforming ways. For some people spiritual direction will lead to political engagement; for others it will mean social action. Some will hear and respond to a call to ordination; others will seek to serve in more hidden but equally transforming ways. Issues of justice and social action are more likely to come to the attention of a group of people who are paying attention to Scripture together. The Psalms, for example, consistently point to questions of justice in the context of the life of the whole community.[7]

Group direction may have a special appeal to young people who want to learn how to listen to God and are used to doing things in groups. Mark Yaconelli developed a discernment process that he described in his book *Contemplative Youth Ministry*.[8] It has a clear structure and involves listening to Scripture and spending time in silence together seeking God's will for decisions and direction. It has echoes of the early Christians in the book of Acts who 'spent much time together' (Acts 2.46). The adoption of a contemplative stance, which is so necessary for the 'noticing' aspect of what the Holy Spirit is up to, especially in a book about youth ministry, is refreshing. Learning to see how God speaks to others, is present to them in different ways and enables us to connect up all the dots of our lives, is something group direction is especially valuable in promoting. It can build confidence where discernment and spiritual wisdom may grow. Although Yaconelli developed this process for youth groups, it is eminently transferable to other contexts. One thinks of parochial church councils and other church business meetings where careful listening to God and to each other could be transformative. Home groups, Lent groups and all kinds of gatherings could be strengthened beyond telling by learning to practise discernment and adopting a more contemplative approach to their tasks.[9]

When we think about being transformed into the likeness of Christ we tend to think in individual terms. What will it be like for me to be like Jesus? What will it be like for someone else? Each one of us will one day be like the Lord and we are already in the process of being transformed. Janet Martin Soskice has explored the Anglo-Saxon word 'kinde', and draws out the root meaning of it in the idea of kinship.[10] The Bible talks about adoption, being children of God and brothers and sisters of Jesus Christ. In God is our collective homecoming where we are accepted and complete, belonging together as family within the godhead. Roger Hurding used the beautiful image of the rose windows found in so many cathedrals, where Christ himself is the complete rose window in all its transmitted glory and we, in our growing Christlikeness, are the individual panes of coloured glass and the tracery that make up the many-petalled rose.[11]

Directors and the Christian community

The communal dimension is also important for directors to consider for their own ministry. Spiritual directors are increasingly being urged to enter into supervision in order to pay attention to their own responses to what they hear. The focus of supervision is not the content of what is said – that is confidential and not the point here. Supervision is to aid awareness of how we as directors respond: what is stirred up in us emotionally, theologically and so on. How open are we to the Holy Spirit? Spiritual directors who avoid being accountable to others and insist on going it alone as free agents should be regarded with caution. We should ask why they refuse to acknowledge the communal aspect of their work both for themselves as directors and their directees as disciples.

Spiritual direction involves a mutual effort to comprehend God and love and follow Christ in this world. It reminds us that we do not undertake this alone. Margaret Guenther describes the work involved as fitting the archetype of Judaeo-Christian truth, that of the Exodus.[12] Like our Jewish forebears we are called to move from slavery to freedom, from Egypt to the Promised Land. We all grow weary on the journey; we have moments of great closeness to God who guides us by a pillar of fire or feeds us with mysterious manna. We have passed dry-shod through some threatening seas. We are tempted time and again to forget the guidance along the way and feel abandoned, alone, confused and wandering. The Jews struggled to remember who they were and whence they had come. They retold the story over and over again to each other so they would never forget God's goodness to them. They bound God's word to their foreheads and to the lintels of their doors. They remembered, celebrated, and built their corporate future based on God's mighty acts on their behalf. Each believing individual mirrors this archetype and we need a believing community to help us interpret our personal story, to see it too as an exodus, to view our private history as sacred history and to be conscious of the covenant God has made and kept with us.

Listening in community

All the examples of communal approaches to discipleship and spiritual direction involve deep listening to others. We have discussed the importance of a relationship with a God who speaks in order to communicate with us, but listening also lies at the heart of this relationship. There is a story that illustrates the close connection with silence and listening. A young man was asked what he was doing when he fell silent in prayer. 'When I am silent I am listening', came his response. 'And what is God doing?' asked his questioner. 'He's listening', said the young man. The God who speaks is also the God who listens. God listens to our praise and delights in it. God also listens to our heart-cries and draws us to the godhead in a gentle caress. God listens to our rage and frustration and takes up our cause. The psalmists expressed every human emotion and threw them all at God with no holds barred. They cried out when they thought God was not listening to them. Sometimes they wondered at the apparent silence. At other times they sang, shouted, cried, lamented, rejoiced because they were confident that God is a God who hears our prayers. We all know what it is like not to be listened to, to be ignored or told to quieten down. Think of the old person who has been abandoned because there is no one to listen to his anxieties; the baby left to cry in her cot; the man with mental health issues who is shunned; the young woman who is confused and too frightened to say what is on her mind. Many of us will have hesitated to ask spiritual leaders for time because they seemed so busy; thus our questions, doubts and longings go unheard. Spiritual direction has listening at its core. We have considered the place of the Holy Spirit as the real director and the importance of both director and directee listening to the Spirit together. Group direction emphasizes the human dimension of this listening process, for it fosters the skill of listening to each other, of giving each other space and time to tell our stories, of building community in the act of listening to another's experience of God, which is not just for themselves alone but for the benefit of the whole body. Together we reconnect our personal story with the biblical story and we help each other practise this neglected gift. As Guenther comments, 'Telling the story restores us to personhood and identity – our true identity in Christ – and thereby restores us to context and context to us.'[13]

11

Conclusion

———•◆•———

'I want more of God in my life' is the heartfelt desire of many Christians in the Church today. Many are longing for a deeper experience of God, one that connects with their real lives. They know there is more but are unsure how to find it. When we open the Scriptures we discover that no matter how long we may have been seeking God, God has been seeking us far longer. How ever much we may want God, the loving Lord wants us far more. God has loved us from eternity, and that love pursues us whether through thunder or a still small voice. At its best, spiritual direction will address some of the questions all of us ask: Who am I? Where am I going? What do I really want? Where do I find hope and meaning? These are very individualistic-sounding questions and all of us are vulnerable to self-deception and to the lies we are fed by a world that does not know God. By ourselves we may easily mistake the siren voices masquerading as truth, so we need companions on the way to guide and direct us, to help us hear the authentic voice of God. When we are tempted to turn our own desires into those of God, a spiritual director can assist us. When we select the parts of Scripture we like and discard the rest, a spiritual director can help us hear the whole counsel of God. When our secret sins threaten to lure us away from God's hand on our lives, a wise director can help us pause and reconsider. We need help to know when to be still and wait, when to get up and act. We need insight into what to read that will speak to us where we are. We need a place to take our questions, our doubts and our puzzlement. Spiritual directors will hold us accountable and encourage us to take spiritual discipline seriously. They will be a prayerful presence and know when to offer a word and when to hold back. They will know God speaking to them through God's word as they ponder it prayerfully for themselves, to be ready to point others to the word. They will be longing for God for themselves and seeking the Lord in their daily lives.

It is this deep-felt desire for God that brings people to seek spiritual direction. Ultimately they are looking for God, though this desire might be cloaked in many guises and expressed in different ways. The Bible is clear that knowing God in every moment is possible and that God is seeking people long before they look for signs of the divine presence. Henri Nouwen liked to draw a line across the blackboard when he was teaching, which he said represented from eternity to eternity. A small space somewhere in the middle represented our lifespan on earth. Long before this brief line began, God loved us, and long after our lives are over, God will go on loving us.[1] Our task in this life is to know the living Word and know we are loved, so that we can love the Lord in return. On every page we are invited to participate in God's purposes, in God's world, in God's reality, which is vast and wonderful – far beyond our wildest imaginings. Karl Barth had a vivid illustration of how this works. Imagine a group of people born in an enclosed space, a warehouse, and who lived there all their lives. There were no entrances or exits but there were some windows, high up and covered in grime. One day one of the children climbed up and looked out. He saw the world outside with people walking about on the street below. He called to his friends to look and as they did so one of the people outside pointed up into the sky and soon a crowd gathered round and all pointed excitedly into the sky. The children inside look up but can only see the roof of their warehouse. After a while the people inside get bored and climb down. Why would those outside get so excited about nothing? What they do not realize is that the people outside are looking up into the sky and seeing all that the heavens contain. What if, one day, the people inside the warehouse cut a way out and went outside and discovered the heavens above for themselves? Barth says that is what happens when we open the Bible.[2] We enter a world that stretches far beyond our dreams, a world of creation and salvation before us, inviting us in. Of course, in all kinds of ways this world is different from the one we know, not least in that God is in control here, not us. It may be safer to stay in our warehouses. For the person who has even a small hunch that there is more, spiritual direction offers a way to explore and push the boundaries of experience Godwards.

There are many options for people who are looking for something more out of life, as well as for those who know they need help of one kind or another. Gary Moon and David Benner have commented that:

> Spiritual direction offers twenty-first-century Christians an ancient and time-honoured relationship of accountability and accompaniment for walking the Christian path. It provides a place within which we can know ourselves as we are truly known. It gives us a place to meet God.[3]

Our culture gives us new words to speak of the Christ we know. Our faith transforms the words coming out of our culture. Spiritual direction can help us find hope in an imperfect world by learning to see things differently, and by wise and judicious use of Scripture it can help to foster a language to see God in all things and articulate our experience with a companion along the way.

Christians believe that the resurrection of Jesus inaugurated a new age. The kingdom of God is here – we are living in it. It has not come fully, but there are signs all around us for those with eyes to see. It is to help people develop such seeing eyes that spiritual directors make themselves available. In this kingdom of truth and grace, healing and new life, the signs are intermingled with many other aspects of the world that do not recognize God's rule. Spiritual deafness and spiritual blindness are everywhere. Their antidote is prayer. Prayer awakens the imagination, sharpens our spiritual eyes and attunes our spiritual ears. Assisting people in their prayer is the greatest privilege imaginable, yet all we are doing is helping them notice the wind of the Spirit as it blows through their existence and transforms it. Countless Christians believe in God and seek to serve the Lord. They are baptized and they long to grow in faith. But they are not aware of where God is at work as they go about their daily business. Spiritual direction helps people redirect their spiritual antennae to detect the signs and spiritual nudges of God and name the Lord's presence. 'For I greet him the days I meet him, and I bless when I understand', said the poet Gerald Manley Hopkins.[4]

There was once a young man who wanted to become a diamond cutter. He was excited because a master craftsman in his chosen career had agreed to take him on as his apprentice. When he arrived at the diamond cutter's workshop on his first day, he was shown into a room with a table and chair. On the table was a diamond. The master craftsman invited him to look at the diamond, closed the door, and left. The next day it was the same, and the day after that. The young man was simply left alone in the room with the diamond on the table. Eventually he rebelled and went home in an angry frame of mind. Recounting his experience that evening he said how he had been left alone in the room day after day with nothing but a diamond on the table. 'And would you believe it?' he exclaimed, 'Today he left me with a fake!'

May God give us eyes to recognize the living Word so that wherever we are we are able to recognize the Lord's footprints and know the divine presence in every part of our lives.

Notes

Preface

1 Richard Foster, *Celebration of Discipline: The Path to Spiritual Growth*, London: Hodder & Stoughton, 1980, p. 1.

1 Introduction: What is spiritual direction?

1 Ralph Martin, *Hungry for God: Practical Help in Personal Prayer*, London: Fontana, 1976.

2 See M. Robert Mulholland, Jr, *The Deeper Journey: The Spirituality of Discovering your True Self*, Downers Grove, IL: InterVarsity Press, 2006, p. 42. Heather Ward explores the concept of self in the light of the Bible and the mystical tradition in *The Gift of Self*, London: Darton, Longman & Todd, 1990.

3 C. S. Lewis, *Mere Christianity*, London: Collins, 1964, p. 175.

4 For an in-depth exploration of this theme, see David Ford, *Self and Salvation: Being Transformed*, Cambridge: Cambridge University Press, 1999.

5 Kenneth Leech, *Soul Friend: A Study of Spirituality*, London: Sheldon Press, 1977, p. 33.

6 By ascetical theology, Leech means 'activity within the body of Christ that seeks to find out and use the methods, techniques and principles which will aid the growth of the life of prayer' (*Soul Friend*, p. 38).

7 Leech, *Soul Friend*, p. 38.

8 Gary W. Moon and David G. Benner (eds), *Spiritual Direction and the Care of Souls: A Guide to Christian Approaches and Practices*, Downers Grove, IL: InterVarsity Press, 2004, p. 245.

9 For a fuller treatment of the theological basis for the encounter with God, see William A. Barry, *Spiritual Direction and the Encounter with God: A Theological Inquiry*, Mahwah, NJ: Paulist Press, 2004.

2 Learning to reflect on our experience

1 Karl Rahner, 'Enthusiasm and Grace', in *Theological Investigations: Experience of the Spirit*, vol. 16, trans. David Morland, New York: Crossroad, 1983, p. 40.

2 Janet K. Ruffing, *Spiritual Direction: Beyond the Beginnings*, New York: Paulist Press, 2000, esp. ch. 3.

3 C. S. Lewis, *Prince Caspian: The Return to Narnia*, London: Puffin, 1963, p. 124.

4 See David Hay and Rebecca Nye, *The Spirit of the Child*, rev. edn, London: Jessica Kingsley, 2006.

5 See David Tracy, *On Naming the Present: Reflections on God, Hermeneutics, and Church*, Maryknoll, NY: Orbis Books; London: SCM Press, 1994, for further discussion of the present as a moment of conflict of interpretations whereby we have modern, antimodern and postmodern ways of describing it. Tracy's hermeneutic emphasizes the analogical imagination.

6 David Tracy, *Blessed Rage for Order: The New Pluralism in Theology – With a New Preface*, Chicago, IL: University of Chicago Press, 1996.

7 Tracy, *Blessed Rage*, p. 136.

8 See, for example, Sue Pickering, *Spiritual Direction: A Practical Introduction*, London: Canterbury Press, 2008; Janet K. Ruffing, *To Tell the Sacred Tale: Spiritual Direction and Narrative*, Mahwah, NJ: Paulist Press, 2011; John Shea, *Stories of God: An Unauthorized Biography*, Chicago, IL: Thomas More Press, 1978.

9 From 'Aurora Leigh', Seventh Book, in *The Poetical Works of Elizabeth Barrett Browning*, Chicago: Belford, Clarke & Co., 1880, p. 452.

10 Kenneth Leech, *Soul Friend: A Study of Spirituality*, London: Sheldon Press, 1977, pp. 36–7.

11 See Walter Brueggemann, 'The Formfulness of Grief', *Interpretation* 31/3, 1977, pp. 263–75.

12 For an invaluable study on the role of Scripture in the lives of the Desert Fathers and Mothers, see Douglas Burton-Christie, *The Word in the Desert: Scripture and the Quest for Holiness in Early Christian Monasticism*, New York: Oxford University Press, 1993.

13 John Calvin, *Institutes of the Christian Religion*, Books I.i–III.xix, Philadelphia, PA: Westminster Press, 1960, p. 35.

14 Nicholas Lash, *Believing Three Ways in One God: A Reading of the Apostles' Creed*, London: SCM Press, 1992, p. 4.

3 The Bible and spiritual direction

1 These writers belong to different denominations but are familiar to the world of spiritual direction.

2 Rowan Williams, Foreword to Enzo Bianchi, *God, Where Are You?*, London: SPCK, 2014.

3 See, for example, Alan Jamieson, *A Churchless Faith: Faith Journeys Beyond the Churches*, London: SPCK, 2002.

4 Kenneth Leech, *Soul Friend: A Study of Spirituality*, London: Sheldon Press, 1977, p. 121.

5 Gordon H. Jeff, *Spiritual Direction for Every Christian*, London: SPCK, 1987.

6 Henri Nouwen, with Michael J. Christensen and Rebecca J. Laird, *Spiritual Direction: Wisdom for the Long Walk of Faith*, London: SPCK, 2011, p. xviii.

7 Margaret Guenther, *Holy Listening: The Art of Spiritual Direction*, London: Darton, Longman & Todd, 1992.

8 Chester P. Michael, *An Introduction to Spiritual Direction: A Psychological Approach for Directors and Directees*, Mahwah, NJ: Paulist Press, 2004.

9 Eugene H. Peterson, *Eat this Book: A Conversation in the Art of Spiritual Reading*, London: Hodder & Stoughton, 2006, p. 4.

10 Alasdair MacIntyre, *After Virtue: A Study in Moral Theory*, Notre Dame, IN: University of Notre Dame Press, 1981, p. 210.

11 See <www.biblereadingnotes.org.uk/quiet-spaces>; <http://bigbible.org.uk/big-read>; <www.walkthru.org>.

12 Dietrich Bonhoeffer, *Life Together*, New York: Harper & Row, 1954, p. 23.

13 Walter Brueggemann, *Redescribing Reality: What We Do When We Read the Bible*, London: SCM Press, 2009, p. 12.

14 Brueggemann, *Redescribing Reality*, p. 13.

15 Brueggemann, *Redescribing Reality*, p. 13.

16 N. T. Wright, *Scripture and the Authority of God*, London: SPCK, 2005, pp. 24–5.

17 Guenther, *Holy Listening*, pp. 44–5.

18 See Edward Farley, *Theologia: The Fragmentation and Unity of Theological Education*, Philadelphia, PA: Fortress Press, 1983.

19 C. S. Lewis, *The Voyage of the Dawn Treader*, London: Puffin, 1963.

20 For more on this theme, see Frances Young, *Virtuoso Theology: The Bible and Interpretation*, Cleveland, OH, Pilgrim Press, 1993, pp. 21–2; Peterson, *Eat this Book*, pp. 76–7; Nicholas Lash, *Theology On the Way to Emmaus*, London: SCM Press, 1986, ch. 3, 'Performing the Scriptures'.

4 The use and abuse of the Bible in spiritual direction

1 Douglas Burton-Christie, *The Word in the Desert: Scripture and the Quest for Holiness in Early Christian Monasticism*, New York: Oxford University Press, 1993, p. 163.

2 Quoted in J. M. Neufelder and M. C. Coelho (eds), *Writings on Spiritual Direction by Great Christian Masters*, New York: Seabury Press, 1982, Epilogue, p. 185.

3 Northrop Frye, *The Great Code: The Bible and Literature*, New York: Harcourt Brace Jovanovich, 1982, p. 208.

4 For his fearfully forbidding picture of 'great uncle George', see Gerard W. Hughes, *God of Surprises*, London: Darton, Longman & Todd, 1985, p. 34.

5 See Richard Rohr, *Things Hidden: Scripture as Spirituality*, Cincinnati, OH: St Anthony Messenger Press, 2008.

6 Frederick Buechner, *Secrets in the Dark: A Life in Sermons*, San Francisco, CA: HarperSanFrancisco, 2006, p. 190.

5 Stories

1 N. T. Wright, *Scripture and the Authority of God*, London: SPCK, 2005, p. 90.

2 Elaine Graham, Heather Walton and Frances Ward, *Theological Reflection: Methods*, London: SCM Press, 2005, pp. 18ff.

3 Henri Nouwen, *The Living Reminder: Service and Prayer in Memory of Jesus Christ*, New York: Seabury Press, 1977, pp. 65–6.

4 Walter Brueggemann, *Redescribing Reality: What We Do When We Read the Bible*, London: SCM Press, 2009, p. xx. Brueggemann goes on to say that biblical exposition is, in the context of the Church, an artistic preoccupation designed to generate alternative futures – something we might consider in the context of spiritual direction also.

5 David Hay and Rebecca Nye, *The Spirit of the Child*, rev. edn, London: Jessica Kingsley, 2006.

6 See Sonja M. Stewart and Jerome W. Berryman, *Young Children and Worship*, Louisville, KY: Westminster John Knox Press, 1989.

7 John Bunyan, 'The Author's Apology for his Book', *The Pilgrim's Progress*, London: Penguin, 2008 (first published 1678).

8 C. S. Lewis, *The Horse and His Boy*, London: Puffin, 1965, p. 170.

9 Rowan Williams, *The Lion's World: A Journey into the Heart of Narnia*, London: SPCK, 2012, ch. 4.

10 Richard Foster, *Prayer: Finding the Heart's True Home*, London: Hodder & Stoughton, 1992, ch. 15.

11 Henri Nouwen, *The Return of the Prodigal Son*, London: Darton, Longman & Todd, 1994.

12 Henry David Thoreau, *Walden*, New York: New American Library, 1960, p. 7.

13 Annie Dillard, *Pilgrim at Tinker Creek*, New York: Harper's Magazine Press, 1974, e.g. pp. 51–3. The whole book is a testimony to careful observation and full of wonder.

6 Themes in Scripture and spiritual direction

1 Janet K. Ruffing, *Spiritual Direction: Beyond the Beginnings*, New York: Paulist Press, 2000.

2 One of the most insightful accounts of a journey in a desert land that is both literal and figurative is Beldon C. Lane, *The Solace of Fierce Landscapes: Exploring Desert and Mountain Spirituality*, New York and Oxford: Oxford University Press, 1998.

3 David Runcorn, *A Spirituality Workbook: A Guide for Explorers, Pilgrims and Seekers*, London: SPCK, 2006, p. 10.

4 Douglas Burton-Christie, *The Word in the Desert: Scripture and the Quest for Holiness in Early Christian Monasticism*, New York: Oxford University Press, 1993, p. 136.

5 Frederick Buechner, *Telling Stories: A Memoir*, New York: HarperCollins, 1991, p. 32.

7 Models of relating in spiritual direction

1 Eugene Peterson, *The Contemplative Pastor: Returning to the Art of Spiritual Direction*, Carol Stream, IL: Christianity Today, 1989, pp. 182ff.

2 Peterson, *Contemplative Pastor*, p. 185.

3 Saying attributed to St Brigid of Kildare.

4 Ignatius of Loyola, *Personal Writings*, ed. Joseph A. Munitiz and Philip Endean, Harmondsworth: Penguin, 1996, Spiritual Exercises 15, p. 286.

5 Quoted in Douglas Burton-Christie, *The Word in the Desert: Scripture and the Quest for Holiness in Early Christian Monasticism*, New York: Oxford University Press, 1993, p. 108.

6 Burton-Christie, *Word in the Desert*, e.g. pp. 23, 61, 135ff.

7 Burton-Christie, *Word in the Desert*, p. 135.

8 Benedicta Ward (trans.), *The Sayings of the Desert Fathers: The Alphabetical Collection*, London: Mowbray, 1975, p. 139.

9 Burton-Christie, *Word in the Desert*, pp. 61–2.

10 See Irénée Hausherr, *Spiritual Direction in the Early Christian East*, trans. Anthony P. Gythiel, Kalamazoo, MI: Cistercian Publications, 1990, Foreword by Bishop Kallistos [Ware] of Diokleia, p. vii.

11 Benedict, *The Rule of St Benedict*, trans. David Parry, OSB, Leominster: Gracewing, 1990, Prologue, p. 1.

12 Friedrich von Hügel, *Selected Letters, 1896–1924*, New York: E. P. Dutton, 1928, p. 229.

13 Eugene H. Peterson, *Eat this Book: A Conversation in the Art of Spiritual Reading*, London: Hodder & Stoughton, 2006, p. 4.

14 David Foster, *Reading with God: Lectio Divina*, London and New York: Continuum, 2005, p. 1.

15 Quoted in Esther de Waal, *A Life-giving Way: A Commentary on the Rule of St. Benedict*, Collegeville, MN: Liturgical Press, 1995, p. 143.

16 Cf. The section 'Holy Scriptures, 1', of George Herbert's poem 'The Sonnet': 'Oh Book! infinite sweetness! let my heart // Suck ev'ry letter, and a honey gain.' George Herbert, *The Complete English Works*, ed. Ann Pasternak Slater, London: Everyman, 1995, p. 56.

17 Foster, *Reading with God*, p. 1.

18 Quoted in David Adam, *Occasions for Alleluia*, London: SPCK, 2012. Based on St Augustine, *The City of God*, trans. John Healey, London: Dent, 1945, vol. 2, p. 408: '... we shall rest and see, we shall see and love, we shall love and we shall praise. Behold what shall be in the end without end.'

19 *The Spiritual Exercises of St Ignatius*, trans. Louis J. Puhl, Chicago, IL: Loyola Press, 1951, p. 15.

20 Gerard W. Hughes, *God of Surprises*, London: Darton, Longman & Todd, 1985.

21 The evangelical understanding of the cross is set out in John R. W. Stott, *The Cross of Christ*, Downers Grove, IL: InterVarsity Press, 1986.

22 See, for example, J. I. Packer, *Keep in Step with the Spirit: Finding Fullness in our Walk with God*, Leicester: Inter-Varsity Press, 1984.

23 See Barry, William A. and Connolly, William J., *The Practice of Spiritual Direction*, New York: Seabury Press, 1982, Janet K. Ruffing, *Spiritual Direction: Beyond the Beginnings*, New York: Paulist Press, 2000. John Bunyan's *Pilgrim's Progress* describes the kind of obstacles to faith that arise.

24 Jeremy Taylor, *Episcopal Charge*, 1661, quoted in Martin Thornton, *English Spirituality: An Outline of Ascetical Theology According to the English Pastoral Tradition*, London: SPCK, 1963, p. 237.

25 George Herbert, *A Priest to the Temple, Or, The Country Parson*, ch. XV, George Herbert, *The Complete English Works*, ed. Slater, p. 219.

26 See, for example, <www.rejesus.co.uk> and <www.churchofengland.org/prayer-worship.aspx>.

27 Quoted in Peter Ball, *Journey into Truth: Spiritual Direction in the Anglican Tradition*, London: Mowbray, 1996, pp. 52–3.

28 Margaret Guenther, *Holy Listening: The Art of Spiritual Direction*, London: Darton, Longman & Todd, 1992.

29 *Teresa of Ávila: The Life of Saint Teresa of Ávila by Herself*, London: Penguin, 1957 (repr. 1987), ch. 11.

30 *St Madeleine Sophie: Her Life and Letters*, quoted in J. M. Neufelder and M. C. Coelho (eds), *Writings on Spiritual Direction by Great Christian Masters*, New York: Seabury Press, 1982, p. 30.

31 Quoted in Hausherr, *Spiritual Direction*, p. xii.

32 *The Spiritual Letters of Dom John Chapman*, quoted in Neufelder and Coelho, *Writings on Spiritual Direction*, p. 31.

33 Quoted in Hausherr, *Spiritual Direction*, p. xiv.

34 See Kenneth Leech, *Soul Friend: A Study of Spirituality*, London: Sheldon Press, 1977; Alan Jones, *Soul Making: The Desert Way of Spirituality*, San Francisco, CA: Harper & Row, 1985; John O'Donoghue, *Anam Chara: Spiritual Wisdom from the Celtic World*, London: Bantam Press, 1997.

35 Aelred of Rievaulx, *Spiritual Friendship*, trans. Mary Eugenia Laker, Kalamazoo, MI: Cistercian Publications, 1977, p. 51.

8 Prayer and praying

1 Henri Nouwen, with Michael J. Christensen and Rebecca J. Laird, *Spiritual Direction: Wisdom for the Long Walk of Faith*, London: SPCK, 2011, pp. 60–1.

2 Henri Nouwen, *From Resentment to Gratitude*, Chicago, IL: Franciscan Herald Press, 1974, p. 30.

3 Eugene H. Peterson, *Eat This Book: A Conversation in the Art of Spiritual Reading*, London: Hodder & Stoughton, pp. 31ff.

4 This story is frequently retold by the Northumbria Community.

5 Eugene Peterson, *The Contemplative Pastor: Returning to the Art of Spiritual Direction*, Carol Stream, IL: Christianity Today, 1989, pp. 90ff.

6 Kathleen Norris suggests, ironically, that the word 'mystic' should carry the same kind of warning as 'poet' when we describe someone as either. Kathleen Norris, *Amazing Grace: A Vocabulary of Faith*, New York: Riverhead Books, 1998, p. 297.

7 Thomas Merton, 'Is mysticism normal?', *Commonweal*, 51 (1949–50), p. 98; cited in John J. Higgins, *Merton's Theology of Prayer*, Spencer, MA: Cistercian Publications, 1971, p. 22.

8 Quoted in Norris: *Amazing Grace*, p. 298.

9 From 'The First Principle and Foundation', commented on in Gerard W. Hughes, *God of Surprises*, London: Darton, Longman & Todd, 1985, p. 59.

10 See, for example, David Kiersey and Marilyn Bates, *Please Understand Me: An Essay on Temperament Styles*, Del Mar, CA: Promethean Books, 1978.

11 See, for example, Ruth Fowke, *Personality and Prayer*, Farnham: CWR, 2008; Chester P. Michael and Marie C. Norrisey: *Prayer and Temperament: Different Prayer Forms for Different Personality Types*, Charlottesville, VA: The Open Door, 1984.

9 Spiritual direction and non-literate approaches to Scripture

1 David Foster, *Reading with God: Lectio Divina*, London and New York: Continuum, 2005, p. 18.

2 Bede, *A History of the English Church and People*, trans. Leo Sherley-Price, Harmondsworth: Penguin, 1955, pp. 246–7.

3 Eugene Peterson, *The Contemplative Pastor: Returning to the Art of Spiritual Direction*, Carol Stream, IL: Christianity Today, 1989, p. 155.

4 Liz Culling and Toddy Hoare, *Sculpture, Prayer and Scripture*, Cambridge: Grove Books, 2004, p. 91.

5 Ann Persson, *The Circle of Love: Praying with Rublev's Icon of the Trinity*, Abingdon: Bible Reading Fellowship, 2010.

10 Alone and together in spiritual direction

1 St Antony, in Benedicta Ward (trans.), *The Sayings of the Desert Fathers: The Alphabetical Collection*, London: Mowbray, 1975, p. 3.

2 Kathleen Norris, *Amazing Grace: A Vocabulary of Faith*, New York: Riverhead Books, 1998, pp. 290–6.

3 Gordon Jeff, *Spiritual Direction for Every Christian*, London: SPCK, 1987, p. 93.

4 Eugene H. Peterson, *Eat this Book: A Conversation in the Art of Spiritual Reading*, London: Hodder & Stoughton, 2006, p. 75.

5 See <www.renovarelife.org>.

6 See <www.northumbriacommunity.org>.

7 See Walter Brueggemann, *The Spirituality of the Psalms*, Minneapolis, MN: Fortress Press, 2002, p. xiii.

8 Mark Yaconelli, *Contemplative Youth Ministry: Practising the Presence of Jesus with Young People*, London: SPCK, 2006.

9 See also other examples in Sue Pickering, *Spiritual Direction: A Practical Introduction*, London: Canterbury Press, 2008, pp. 194ff.

10 Janet Martin Soskice, *The Kindness of God: Metaphor, Gender and Religious Language*, Oxford: Oxford University Press, 2007.

11 Roger Hurding, *Five Pathways to Wholeness: Explorations in Pastoral Care and Counselling*, London: SPCK, 2013, p. 140.

12 Margaret Guenther, *Holy Listening: The Art of Spiritual Direction*, London: Darton, Longman & Todd, 1992, p. 7.

13 Guenther, *Holy Listening*, p. 149.

11 Conclusion

1 Henri Nouwen, with Michael J. Christensen and Rebecca J. Laird, *Spiritual Direction: Wisdom for the Long Walk of Faith*, London: SPCK, 2011, p. 38.

2 Karl Barth, 'The Strange New World Within the Bible', in *The Word of God and the Word of Man*, Gloucester, MA: Peter Smith, 1978 [first published 1928], pp. 28–50.

3 Gary W. Moon and David G. Benner (eds), *Spiritual Direction and the Care of Souls: A Guide to Christian Approaches and Practices*, Downers Grove, IL: InterVarsity Press, 2004, p. 300.

4 'The Wreck of the Deutschland', stanza 5, in *The Poems of Gerard Manley Hopkins*, 4th edn, ed. W. H. Gardner and N. H. MacKenzie, London: Oxford University Press, 1970, p. 53.

Bibliography

Aelred of Rievaulx, *Spiritual Friendship*, trans. Mary Eugenia Laker, Kalamazoo, MI: Cistercian Publications, 1977.

Ball, Peter, *Journey into Truth: Spiritual Direction in the Anglican Tradition*, London: Mowbray, 1996.

Barry, William A., *Spiritual Direction and the Encounter with God: A Theological Enquiry*, Mahwah, NJ: Paulist Press, 2004.

Barry, William A. and Connolly, William J., *The Practice of Spiritual Direction*, New York: Seabury Press, 1982.

Barth, Karl, 'The Strange New World Within the Bible', in *The Word of God and the Word of Man*, Gloucester, MA: Peter Smith, 1978 [first published 1928].

Bede, *A History of the English Church and People*, trans. Leo Sherley-Price, Harmondsworth: Penguin, 1955.

Benedict, *The Rule of Saint Benedict*, trans. Abbot Parry, OSB, Leominster: Gracewing, 1990.

Bianchi, Enzo, *God, Where Are You?* London: SPCK, 2014.

Bonhoeffer, Dietrich, *Life Together*, trans. John W. Doberstein, New York: Harper, 1954.

Book of Common Prayer, Cambridge: Cambridge University Press, 2004.

Browning, Elizabeth Barrett, *The Poetical Works of Elizabeth Barrett Browning*, Chicago, IL: Belford, Clarke & Co., 1880.

Brueggemann, Walter, 'The Formfulness of Grief', *Interpretation* 31/3, 1977.

Brueggemann, Walter, *The Spirituality of the Psalms*, Minneapolis, MN: Fortress Press, 2002.

Brueggemann, Walter, *Redescribing Reality: What We Do When We Read the Bible*, London: SCM Press, 2009.

Buechner, Frederick, *Telling Stories: A Memoir*, New York: HarperCollins, 1991.

Buechner, Frederick, *Secrets in the Dark: A Life in Sermons*, San Francisco, CA: HarperSanFrancisco, 2006.

Bunyan, John, *The Pilgrim's Progress*, London: Penguin, 2008 (first published 1678).

Burton-Christie, Douglas, *The Word in the Desert: Scripture and the Quest for Holiness in Early Christian Monasticism*, New York: Oxford University Press, 1993.

Calvin, John, *Institutes of the Christian Religion*, ed. John McNeill, 2 vols, Philadelphia, PA: Westminster Press, 1960.

Conroy, Maureen, *Looking into the Well: Supervision of Spiritual Directors*, Chicago, IL: Loyola University Press, 1995.

Culling, Liz and Hoare, Toddy, *Sculpture, Prayer and Scripture*, Cambridge: Grove Books, 2004.

De Waal, Esther, *A Life-giving Way: A Commentary on the Rule of St Benedict*, Collegeville, MN: Liturgical Press, 1995.

Dillard, Annie, *Pilgrim at Tinker Creek*, New York: Harper's Magazine Press, 1974.

Farley, Edward, *Theologia: The Fragmentation and Unity of Theological Education*, Philadelphia, PA: Fortress Press, 1983.

Ford, David, *Self and Salvation: Being Transformed*, Cambridge: Cambridge University Press, 1999.

Foster, David, *Reading with God: Lectio Divina*, London and New York: Continuum, 2005.

Foster, Richard, *Celebration of Discipline: The Path to Spiritual Growth*, London: Hodder & Stoughton, 1980.

Foster, Richard, *Prayer: Finding the Heart's True Home*, London: Hodder & Stoughton, 1992.

Fowke, Ruth, *Personality and Prayer*, Farnham: CWR, 2008.

Frye, Northrop, *The Great Code: The Bible and Literature*, New York: Harcourt Brace Jovanovich, 1982.

Gardner, W. H. and MacKenzie, N. H. (eds), *The Poems of Gerard Manley Hopkins*, 4th edn, London: Oxford University Press, 1970.

Graham, Elaine, Walton, Heather and Ward, Frances, *Theological Reflection: Methods*, London: SCM Press, 2005.

Guenther, Margaret, *Holy Listening: The Art of Spiritual Direction*, London: Darton, Longman & Todd, 1992.

Hausherr, Irénée, *Spiritual Direction in the Early Christian East*, trans. Anthony P. Gythiel, Kalamazoo, MI: Cistercian Publications, 1990.

Hay, David and Nye, Rebecca, *The Spirit of the Child*, rev. edn, London: Jessica Kingsley, 2006.

Herbert, George, *The Complete English Works*, ed. Ann Pasternak Slater, London: Everyman, 1995.

Higgins, John J., *Merton's Theology of Prayer*, Spencer, MA: Cistercian Publications, 1971.

Hughes, Gerard W., *God of Surprises*, London: Darton, Longman & Todd, 1985.

Hurding, Roger, *Five Pathways to Wholeness: Explorations in Pastoral Care and Counselling*, London: SPCK, 2013.

Ignatius of Loyola, *The Spiritual Exercises of St Ignatius*, trans. Louis J. Puhl, Chicago, IL: Loyola Press, 1951.

Ignatius of Loyola, *Personal Writings*, ed. Joseph A. Munitiz and Philip Endean, Harmondsworth: Penguin, 1996.

Jamieson, Alan, *A Churchless Faith: Faith Journeys Beyond the Churches*, London: SPCK, 2002.

Jeff, Gordon, *Spiritual Direction for Every Christian*, London: SPCK, 1987.

Jones, Alan, *Soul Making: The Desert Way of Spirituality*, San Francisco, CA: Harper & Row, 1985.

Kiersey, David and Bates, Marilyn: *Please Understand Me: An Essay on Temperament Styles*, Del Mar, CA: Promethean Books, 1978.

Lane, Belden C., *The Solace of Fierce Landscapes: Exploring Desert and Mountain Spirituality*, New York and Oxford: Oxford University Press, 1998.

Lash, Nicholas, 'Performing the Scriptures', in *Theology on the Way to Emmaus*, London: SCM Press, 1986.

Lash, Nicholas, *Believing Three Ways in One God: A Reading of the Apostles' Creed*, London: SCM Press, 1992.

Leech, Kenneth, *Soul Friend: A Study of Spirituality*, London: Sheldon Press, 1977.

Lewis, C. S., *Prince Caspian: The Return to Narnia*, London: Puffin, 1963.

Lewis, C. S., *The Voyage of the Dawn Treader*, London: Puffin, 1963.

Lewis, C. S., *Mere Christianity*, London: Collins, 1964.

Lewis, C. S., *The Horse and His Boy*, Puffin, 1965.

MacIntyre, Alasdair, *After Virtue: A Study in Moral Theory*, Notre Dame, IN: University of Notre Dame Press, 1981.

Martin, Ralph, *Hungry for God: Practical Help in Personal Prayer*, London: Fontana, 1976.

May, Gerald, *Care of Mind, Care of Spirit: A Psychiatrist Explores Spiritual Direction*, San Francisco, CA: HarperSanFrancisco, 1982.

Michael, Chester P., *An Introduction to Spiritual Direction: A Psychological Approach for Directors and Directees*, Mahwah, NJ: Paulist Press, 2004.

Michael, Chester P. and Norrisey, Marie C., *Prayer and Temperament: Different Prayer Forms for Different Personality Types*, Charlottesville, VA: The Open Door, 1984.

Moon, Gary W. and Benner, David G. (eds), *Spiritual Direction and the Care of Souls: A Guide to Christian Approaches and Practices*, Downers Grove, IL: InterVarsity Press, 2004.

Mulholland, M. Robert, Jr, *The Deeper Journey: The Spirituality of Discovering your True Self*, Downers Grove, IL: InterVarsity Press, 2006.

Neufelder, J. M. and Coelho, M .C. (eds), *Writings on Spiritual Direction by Great Christian Masters*, New York: Seabury Press, 1982.

Norris, Kathleen, *Amazing Grace: A Vocabulary of Faith*, New York: Riverhead Books, 1998.

Northumbria Community, *Celtic Daily Prayer: From the Northumbria Community*, rev. edn, London: HarperCollins, 2005.

Nouwen, Henri, *From Resentment to Gratitude*, Chicago, IL: Franciscan Herald Press, 1974.

Nouwen, Henri, *The Living Reminder: Service and Prayer in Memory of Jesus Christ*, New York: Seabury Press, 1977.

Nouwen, Henri, with Christensen, Michael J. and Laird, Rebecca J., *The Return of the Prodigal Son*, London: Darton, Longman & Todd, 1994.

Nouwen, Henri, *Spiritual Direction: Wisdom for the Long Walk of Faith*, London: SPCK, 2011.

O'Donoghue, John, *Anam Chara: Spiritual Wisdom from the Celtic World*, London: Bantam Press, 1997.

Packer, J. I., *Keep in Step with the Spirit: Finding Fullness in Our Walk with God*, Leicester: Inter-Varsity Press, 1984.

Patrides, C. A. (ed.), *The English Poems of George Herbert*, London: Dent, 1974.

Persson, Ann, *The Circle of Love: Praying with Rublev's Icon of the Trinity*, Abingdon: Bible Reading Fellowship, 2010.

Peterson, Eugene, *The Contemplative Pastor: Returning to the Art of Spiritual Direction*, Carol Stream, IL: Christianity Today, 1989.

Peterson, Eugene, *Eat this Book: A Conversation in the Art of Spiritual Reading*, London: Hodder & Stoughton, 2006.

Pickering, Sue, *Spiritual Direction: A Practical Introduction*, London: Canterbury Press, 2008.

Rahner, Karl, 'Enthusiasm and Grace', in *Theological Investigations: Experience of the Spirit*, trans. David Morland, trans. David Morland, New York: Crossroad, 1983.

Rohr, Richard, *Things Hidden: Scripture as Spirituality*, Cincinnati, OH: St Anthony Messenger Press, 2008.

Ruffing, Janet K., *Spiritual Direction: Beyond the Beginnings*, New York: Paulist Press, 2000.

Ruffing, Janet K., *To Tell the Sacred Tale: Spiritual Direction and Narrative*, Mahwah, NJ: Paulist Press, 2011.

Runcorn, David, *A Spirituality Workbook: A Guide for Explorers, Pilgrims and Seekers*, London: SPCK, 2006.

Shea, John, *Stories of God: An Unauthorized Biography*, Chicago, IL: Thomas More Press, 1978.

Soskice, Janet Martin, *The Kindness of God: Metaphor, Gender and Religious Language*, Oxford: Oxford University Press, 2007.

Stewart, Sonja M. and Berryman, Jerome W., *Young Children and Worship*, Louisville, KY: Westminster John Knox Press, 1989.

Stott, John R. W., *The Cross of Christ*, Downers Grove, IL: InterVarsity Press, 1986.

Taylor, Jeremy, *The Rule and Exercises of Holy Living* (1650), ed. P. G. Stanwood, Oxford: Clarendon Press, 1989; *The Rule and Exercises of Holy Dying* (1651), ed. P. G. Stanwood, Oxford: Clarendon Press, 1989.

Teresa of Ávila: *The Life of Saint Teresa of Ávila by Herself*, trans. J. M. Cohen, London: Penguin, 1957 (repr. 1987).

Thomas à Kempis, *The Imitation of Christ*, London: Chapman & Hall, 1910.

Thoreau, Henry David, *Walden*, New York: New American Library, 1960.

Thornton, Martin, *English Spirituality: An Outline of Ascetical Theology According to the English Pastoral Tradition*, London: SPCK, 1963.

Tracy, David, *On Naming the Present: Reflections on God, Hermeneutics, and Church*, Maryknoll, NY: Orbis Books; London: SCM Press, 1994.

Tracy, David, *Blessed Rage for Order: The New Pluralism in Theology – With a New Preface*, Chicago, IL: University of Chicago Press, 1996.

Von Hügel, Friedrich, *Selected Letters, 1896–1924*, New York: E. P. Dutton, 1928.

Ward, Benedicta (trans.), *The Sayings of the Desert Fathers: The Alphabetical Collection*, London: Mowbray, 1975.

Ward, Heather, *The Gift of Self*, London: Darton, Longman & Todd, 1990.

Williams, Rowan, *The Lion's World: A Journey into the Heart of Narnia*, London: SPCK, 2012.

Wright, N. T., *Scripture and the Authority of God*, London: SPCK, 2005.

Yaconelli, Mark, *Contemplative Youth Ministry: Practising the Presence of Jesus with Young People*, London: SPCK, 2006.

Young, Frances, *Virtuoso Theology: The Bible and Interpretation*, Cleveland, OH: Pilgrim Press, 1993.

Internet resources

www.sacredspace.ie
www.rejesus.co.uk
www.churchofengland.org/prayer-worship.aspx

Index

9 780819 232571